THE PREVENTION OF NUCLEAR WAR

The Prevention of Nuclear War

A United States Approach

William H. Lewis

Director, Security Policy Studies
The George Washington University

Oelgeschlager, Gunn & Hain, Publishers, Inc.
Boston, Massachusetts

International Standard Book Number: 0-89946-206-5

Library of Congress Catalog Card Number: 85-15580

Printed in the U.S.A.

Library of Congress Cataloging-in-Publication Data

Lewis, William Hubert, 1928-
  The prevention of nuclear war.

  Includes bibliographic references.
  1. Nuclear disarmament–United States.
2. Nuclear arms control. I. Title.
JX1974.7.L36 1985   327.1'74   85-15580
ISBN 0-89946-206-5

U.N. Sales Number E.85.XV.RR/32

Contents

Foreword   vii

Chapter 1   **Introduction**   1

Chapter 2   **Basic Means of Preventing Nuclear War**
Nonuse of Nuclear Weapons
Detente, Deterrence, and Crisis
    Management
Building Mutual Trust and Confidence   13

Chapter 3   **Conventional Arms in a World
    of Conflict**
Reduction of Conflict
The Correlation of Conventional and
    Nuclear War
The Need for Dialogue   37

Chapter 4   **The Nonproliferation of
    Nuclear Weapons**   49

Chapter 5   **The Role of Nongovernmental
    Organizations**   59

Chapter 6   **Conclusion**   69

Appendix A   **Address by President Reagan Before
    the Thirty-Ninth Session of the
    United Nations General Assembly,
    September 24, 1984**   71

Appendix B   **Text on the Nonproliferation
    Treaty, 1968**   81

Appendix C   **Treaty for the Prohibition of Nuclear
    Weapons in Latin America, 1967**   88

About the Author   103

Foreword

This book is one of three studies the United Nations Institute for Training and Research (UNITAR) is devoting to the prevention of nuclear war. The project under which the three studies were launched was initiated in 1982 in response to recommendations by the United Nations General Assembly that UNITAR focus greater attention on studies dealing with international peace and security, disarmament, and the prevention of nuclear war.

It was decided that three manuscripts be produced: one from a United Nations perspective, one from a United States perspective, and one to reflect the viewpoint of Soviet scientists. The first and last of these studies have been published previously. The three studies constitute a trilogy that is intended to provide comprehensive coverage of the problem of preventing nuclear war.

The research project in its entirety was envisaged as a means for analyzing a subject of fundamental interest to the cause of world peace—the threat of a nuclear war—and of possible ways to avert it. The research deals with the issues related to the development, production, deployment, and use of nuclear weapons and with the measures proposed for preventing the proliferation of these weapons by the nuclear and nonnuclear powers and for halting and reversing the nuclear arms race.

The world today is faced with an escalating arms race and the threat of possible nuclear war. Intensive new efforts are necessary to remove the threat of war, to preserve international security, and to impart insight into the positions of all the primary actors who influence our security. This volume has been prepared by an expert from the United States in the field of disarmament and reflects the United States perspective. It is hoped that, together with the other two volumes already published by UNITAR, it will constitute an important contribution to the understanding of questions that are basic to human survival.

The views and conclusions in this book are the responsibility of the author and do not necessarily reflect the opinions of UNITAR or its Board of Trustees. Although UNITAR takes no position on the views and conclusions expressed by the authors of its studies, it does assume responsibility for determining whether a study merits publication.

MICHEL DOO KINGUÉ
Executive Director

Chapter 1

Introduction

It is now almost four decades since humankind has entered the nuclear age. During this period, innumerable conferences and colloquia have been convened to discuss and to urge nuclear disarmament – the reflection of a profound yearning to free the community of nations from the dangers of nuclear war. The United Nations has been in the forefront of the drive to diminish the likelihood of such a cataclysm, as was witnessed in the tenth special session of the United Nations General Assembly in mid-1978. In its Final Document, the participants agreed on the urgent need to remove "the threat of a world war – a nuclear war" and concluded with the solemn and deeply disturbing observation: "Mankind is confronted with a choice: we must halt the arms race and proceed to disarmament or face annihilation."[1]

Since the convening of the special session on disarmament, various Member States of the United Nations have reaffirmed their desire to improve prospects for nuclear disarmament. A wide variety of measures have been proposed, ranging from an initial freeze on the deployment of all new weapons systems to a systematic build-down of existing inventories, with the ultimate goal of achieving zero inventories. The United States and the Soviet Union, the principal nations concerned, have advanced several proposals consonant with the wishes of the Member States. Nevertheless, very little progress has been registered in the area of nuclear disarmament since the convening of the tenth special session of the United Nations General Assembly in 1978.

The nuclear weapons inventories of the United States and the Soviet Union continue to be enlarged, with the likelihood that ongoing competition will lead to the erosion of previously concluded international understandings and agreements. Moreover, other Member States that possess nuclear weapons arsenals, following the example of the two so-called superpowers, have embarked on programs of weapons modernization. Equally troubling are clear indications that a number of nations that do not at present possess such weapons have initiated research programs and related activities that suggest they intend to enter the ranks of the nuclear weapons "club."

These actions have been undertaken at a time when all Member States acknowledge that conflict between nuclear powers could prove catastrophic for international society. As Michael Mandelbaum has written:

> A nuclear war would destroy not only lives but in all likelihood a way of life. Modern societies are not composed of isolated groups of people in autonomous settlements, but of networks that knit them together on a large scale. The citizens of modern societies do not rely on themselves for food, water, shelter, and transportation. They depend on millions of others. Nuclear war would shatter the networks that support modern existence.[2]

Dr. Mandelbaum has also observed:

> [Nuclear war] poses an even greater threat—not only to our modern way of life, but to life itself. It might alter not only the social but the natural environment. The climate, the soil, the atmosphere that shields living things from the full force of the sun's rays might all be damaged. A particular combination of conditions makes life possible on the planet earth. Nuclear war, unlike any war of the past, could change these conditions.[3]

These potential consequences have been confirmed and reaffirmed by eminent scientists and research scholars throughout the community of nations. In December 1983, a group of Soviet and U.S. scientists met in the caucus room of the U.S. Senate to discuss their separate findings. Based on an assessment of emerging data about the probable climatic, biological, and environmental effects of a nuclear war, a large-scale exchange would mean the extinction of the human race. Indeed, an exchange even using a small number of existing warheads would produce a so-called nuclear winter in which sunlight would be obscured, temperatures would be plunged to below freezing levels in summer, food crops and other ecological systems would be destroyed, and the possibility of a toxic fog encompassing the planet might materialize. As the scientists who convened in Washington, D.C., observed, a nuclear attack would be suicidal for the nation that launched it, even if there were no retaliatory response. Equally clear to the scientists was the inescapable conclusion that the "whole of the earth and human civilization . . . are held hostage" to a situation in which nuclear disarmament is not achieved because there can be no sanctuaries from the consequences of nuclear war.[4]

Prior to the nuclear age, nations embarked on armed conflict because victory in the form of territorial gain, ideological domination, or some other form of advantage seemed possible. The nuclear age has placed in doubt the very notion of victory; material gain cannot be vouchsafed through the launching of nuclear warheads against an adversary. Indeed, even the traditional concept of war must undergo revision since war implies the use of deadly instruments to achieve well-defined political purposes. No meaningful political purpose can be identified when the consequence of a nuclear conflict is the death of hundreds of millions of human beings and the destruction of whole societies—indeed, world civilization as it is presently known.

Every U.S. president, from Harry S. Truman in 1945 to Ronald Reagan in 1985, has been cognizant of the grave responsibilities that are imposed on nations possessing nuclear arsenals to prevent a nuclear holocaust. As a major architect in the formation of the United Nations, the United States subscribed without reservation to the Charter of the United Nations—which was signed June 25, 1945, and came into effect October 25, 1945—a key provision of which accords primary responsibility for maintaining international peace and providing collective security to the Security Council, particularly its five permanent members. The explosion of the first nuclear bomb on July 16, 1945, produced a special urgency to the question of prevention of war. To address the totally unprecedented issues raised by nuclear weapons, the General Assembly created the United Nations Atomic Energy Commission (January 1946), composed of representatives of all nations on the Security Council and Canada.[5] The U.S. government, shortly after the creation of the United Nations Atomic Energy Commission, tabled a series of constructive proposals before that body. Referred to as the Baruch Plan (after Bernard Baruch, its primary sponsor), the U.S. government offered to transfer to the United Nations full information about nuclear technology and full control over sources of raw materials, as well as means of production, provided that the veto power of the permanent members of the Security Council be abrogated in enforcement decisions relating to the development and control of atomic energy. In addition, the United States required that an international atomic development authority be created with powers to control and inspect all atomic activities throughout the community of nations.

As is well known, the Baruch Plan was vigorously opposed, and ultimately rejected, by the Soviet Union. The Soviet position, as stated by its representative in the Atomic Energy Commission, was that the United Nations was not an objective or trustworthy body since it has served from the date of its formation as an organ of U.S. power. Objecting in particular to the provisions of the plan calling for abrogation of veto powers and internationally supervised inspection of atomic activities, the Soviet representative indicated that his government viewed these proposals as stratagems intended to diminish Soviet influence in the United Nations, as well as representing a blatant effort to undermine Soviet sovereignty. In September 1949, the Soviet Union tested its first atomic device, thereby ending the U.S. monopoly in the field and producing effectively the demise of the Baruch Plan. The United Nations Atomic Energy Commission was to collapse shortly thereafter over a dispute wholly unrelated to matters concerning nuclear disarmament–the refusal of the Soviet Union to participate in the commission's deliberations unless and until Nationalist China (Taiwan) was replaced at the United Nations by a representative of the People's Republic of China.

The efforts of the members of the commission to find a formula for nuclear disarmament aborted at a time when the weapons inventories of the United States and the Soviet Union were exceedingly slender. An opportunity was lost that now appears almost irretrievable. Since 1950, the arsenals of both nations have expanded prodigiously–their total now exceeding 40,000 warheads, including tactical, theater, and strategic weapons systems. Both nations at present preside over inventories that have destructive capabilities that exceed those of all the peoples and nations combined since the origins of humankind. These nuclear weapons, moreover, can be delivered over greater distances, with greater accuracy and kill potential than was ever imagined possible in the first decade of the nuclear age. Both the United States and the Soviet Union have mastered the mysteries of inertial guidance, solid fuel propellants, multiple warheading, rocketry trajectory, and hundreds of other scientific and technological variants that insure the ability to visit unimagined destruction on one another. And, the competition in the field of research and development to achieve temporary military advantage continues, with special emphasis on particle beam systems, outer space weaponry, and new generations of mobile strategic weapons delivery systems.

The Member States of the United Nations have been unhappy witness to this unfolding process, urging through various forums and conferences a deceleration of the process of arms competition, one which clearly threatens the stability and well-being of all of humankind. The record of accomplishment has not been without distinction. The United Nations has played a signal role in providing a venue for discussions on disarmament and a center for urging renewed efforts at bilateral negotiations between the United States and the Soviet Union.

After the initial failure at comprehensive nuclear disarmament, as represented by the Baruch Plan, both governments moved cautiously over the next two decades to explore the feasibility of more limited measures. The search for a basis for confidence building centered during the 1950s on atomic testing. Fear of toxic radioactive fallout that could contaminate international society focused the minds of U.S. and Soviet leaders during this period and led them in 1963 to conclude a treaty that prohibited testing in the atmosphere, in outer space, and beneath the oceans. The Limited Test Ban Treaty, which unfortunately did not proscribe all underground testing, provided the impetus needed to produce agreement in other weapons fields (Table 1–1). The most important of these was the Nonproliferation Treaty of 1968, a significant effort organized jointly by the United States and the Soviet Union, which sought to secure agreement by nonnuclear weapons nations to foreswear efforts to acquire such weaponry. (One hundred nineteen of the 159 United Nations Member States have adhered to the treaty.)

In the 1970s, the two superpowers undertook the Strategic Arms Limitation Talks (SALT), which produced several major agreements—in particular, a freeze on certain land- and submarine-based ballistic missile systems and a treaty effectively prohibiting ballistic missile defense. In 1979, the two governments concluded a SALT II agreement that imposed even more stringent limits on certain types of weapons systems and, while the agreement has not been ratified by the United States, both President Carter and his successor, President Reagan, pledged to abide by its provisions. In the interim, U.S. and Soviet negotiators have embarked on a third round of strategic arms limitation negotiations designated by President Reagan as START, the acronym for Strategic Arms Reduction Talks.

Arms control and disarmament have not been purely technical initiatives by the U.S. government. An important component in the U.S. approach has been a sincere desire to diminish tensions and to find a basis for accommodation between Washington and Moscow. The arms control policies of the United States have been a balanced mixture of hope, expectations, and realism. Successive U.S. presidents have viewed arms control negotiations as an opportunity to test the willingness of the Soviet Union to set aside ideological considerations and imperial ambitions in favor of international stability and orderly social and political change. To date, U.S. hopes and expectations have not been realized. The Soviet policy of support for revolutionary movements has generated widening doubt in the United States concerning the basic goals and motivations of the Soviet leadership. Nowhere is this more clearly underscored than in the field of nuclear weaponry, where the Soviet Union moved during the 1970s to secure significant military advantages over the United States. The following data (which I have compiled personally) supports this perception of Soviet capabilities and intentions:

1. The Soviet Union produced more than 2,000 new warheads for strategic weapons; by comparison, the United States built approximately 350 during the same time frame.
2. The Soviet Union launched 61 attack submarines; the United States, 27.
3. The Soviet Union has conducted the first tests of two new land-based intercontinental ballistic missiles in apparent violation of the provisions of SALT II; at the same time it is flight testing a new generation of strategic bombers that is expected to become operational over the next several years.
4. The first units of a 25,000-ton Typhoon-class strategic ballistic missile submarine, the largest in the world, are now in the process of deployment.

The Soviet military sector continues to have the highest claim on the Soviet budget, raw materials, transportation resources, personnel, and capital equipment. More than one-third of all Soviet machinery output now goes to its military sector, and approximately one-half of all research and development expenditures are for military applications. In human terms, the Soviet military sector accounts for one-seventh of total labor-power resources and a substantially higher portion of the best qualified scientific and technical specialists. No other Member State of the United Nations can lay claim to such resources for military purposes – or, in the words of one U.S. president, "war making."[6]

The United States is not the only nation to be impressed by the weight and capabilities of the Soviet military establishment. Nations in Western Europe and the Far East have become deeply disturbed by the deployment of a new theater nuclear weapons system, the SS-20, which is mobile, has an extended range, is multiple warheaded, and is highly accurate. Despite assurances by Leonid Brezhnev to Chancellor Schmidt of West Germany in the mid-1970s that the SS-20 would be introduced in limited numbers – and later assurances that deployments had ceased – the Soviet government has continued its deployment of the intermediate-range system. By 1983, more than two-thirds of the estimated total of 369 SS-20 launchers were aimed at Western Europe. Despite repeated appeals for a cessation of deployment and the opening of bilateral talks between the United States and the Soviet Union in November 1981 to reach agreement, Soviet deployments in Europe continued and even accelerated in 1982 in the face of official Soviet promises to the contrary. Faced with Soviet efforts at political intimidation, the North Atlantic Treaty Organization (NATO) agreed to deployment of a limited number of cruise and Pershing II systems to offset the superiority in intermediate-range nuclear systems enjoyed by the Soviet Union. This act led the Soviet Union to walk out of the negotiations with the United States conducted at Geneva, Switzerland, and to announce that it would accelerate the pace of planned deployments of tactical nuclear systems in Europe as well as increase the size and capabilities of strategic weapons positioned aboard submarines adjacent to U.S. coastal waters. At approximately the same time, Soviet delegations removed themselves from talks being conducted on strategic weapons (START) ostensibly in retaliation for the NATO decision on cruise missiles and Pershing II.

Soviet actions of negative consequence come at a time when its official representatives provide a chorus of vows and protestation in support of peaceful coexistence, confidence building, and nuclear disarmament. Unfortunately, the actual performance of the Soviet Union is at variance with the rhetoric of its representatives in the United Nations and elsewhere. For example, speaking at the United Nations General Assembly's second special session on disarmament, the then Soviet Foreign Minister, Andrei Gromyko, declaimed:

> A genuine desire for peace requires the maintenance of the military-strategic balance. . . . So would it not be better to use it as a springboard from which to work towards agreement to lower its levels in accordance with the principle of equality and equal security?[7]

President Reagan has fully subscribed to this view, as evidenced by his announcement that the START negotiations, which began on May 9, 1982, would, it was hoped, underwrite a basic U.S. goal—not simply to freeze but also to reduce the deployment of weapons capable of nuclear destruction without endangering the security of the United States. The president's initial START proposal included substantial reductions in the existing inventories of Soviet and U.S. intercontinental ballistic missiles and submarine-launched ballistic missiles. Each nation would be permitted to deploy the same number of these weapons until complete disarmament is achieved. In November 1981, consonant with this approach, President Reagan also recommended that negotiators at Geneva addressing theater nuclear weapons also agree that their ultimate goal be reductions of arsenals to the zero inventory level. The Soviet Union objected almost immediately to both proposals, once again placing in doubt its declared disarmament objectives.

Soviet behavior, in the nonnuclear field, despite its disturbing impact on U.S. national interests, has not dissuaded the U.S. government from continuing its search for a basis for arms control agreement. A number of U.S. officials have argued that negotiations on nuclear matters are too important to be derailed by political factors that impact adversely on the climate of international opinion or on U.S. interests. However, the vicissitudes of Soviet foreign policy behavior almost unavoidably cast a cloud over all arms control negotiations since mutual trust and confidence must form the bedrock for successful treaty execution. Thus, both parties, if nuclear war is to be prevented, must exercise a greater degree of self-restraint in both the political and military spheres. Lack of trust has grown perceptibly in recent years, and the atmosphere of relations between the United States and the Soviet Union is most unsettled at the present time.

The leaders of both nations acknowledge the imperative for peace that exists in a nuclear world. They also acknowledge that war between the United States and the Soviet Union would be suicidal under any circumstances. Thus, some measure of mutual restraint is to be expected when sensitive issues arise between the two superpowers. For the future, the principal questions they confront are as follows: (1) How do the two nations maintain strategic stability while once again embarking on purposeful arms control and disarmament negotiations? (2) What degree of national sovereignty and pride are the two governments prepared to sacrifice in the cause of nuclear war prevention? (3) What roles can various international organizations play in facilitating superpower negotiations and encouraging other nations to adhere to the provisions of the Nonproliferation Treaty? As one informed observer has noted:

> If the agreements of the future follow the pattern of the past, they will have an odd feature. The impulse for negotiated agreements comes from the fear of nuclear war. Preventing nuclear war was the aim of the original disarmament scheme, which gave rise to the "first step" approach, which in turn led to negotiations that the United States and the Soviet Union have been holding for over a quarter of a century. Preventing nuclear war is the reason that the American president—as well, perhaps, as his Soviet counterpart—invariably has become a partisan of nuclear negotiations.[8]

More than a quarter-century of negotiations between the United States and the Soviet Union has produced an impressive list of agreements in a number of fields, ranging from nuclear weaponry to commercial accords. Nevertheless, in 1985, the two nations are not prepared to take the ultimate risk to sovereignty and security by concluding an agreement on immediate nuclear disarmament. The basic reason reposes in the profound disagreement that exists in the political realm—a realm where confidence building is frustrated by the seeming incompatibility of the social systems and political orientations of the two nuclear superpowers.

Since political conflicts are the essential precipitants of armed conflict, additional attention must be devoted in this area in the search for institutionalizing the processes that insure peaceful resolution of disputes. This is not to suggest that arms control is not an important adjunct to nuclear war prevention. Quite obviously, processes of negotiation and agreement, even in limited fields, are important symbols of cooperation that can provide the foundations for nuclear peace. They achieve the highest degree of importance, however, only when they are accompanied by political consensus and agreement to accommodate national interests to the clearly expressed desires of the world community to find the means for the prevention of nuclear war.

Where superpower interests are concerned, it must be recognized that the principal imperative is to avoid all forms of confrontation and conflict. The distinction that is often made between recourse to conventional war and nuclear war is both artificial and unverifiable. The risks associated in any military collisions at the lowest level of the spectrum are too great to accept given the size of existing nuclear arsenals and the uncertainty that surrounds circumstances in which a major power will feel under compulsion to execute its nuclear option. Similarly, where superpowers adopt the strategy of proxy wars—including wars of national liberation—national prestige and national pride might well lead to direct involvement. The incidence of such conflicts has risen markedly over the past decade and also must become a matter of increased concern to the United Nations if war prevention—nuclear and nonnuclear—is to be a realistic goal of the international community.

Confidence building, then, must be a multidimensional, continuous process of mutual accommodation. The process must operate at different levels—bilateral and multilateral—simultaneously and must encompass nongovernmental organizations as well as official organs. It must address a number of agendas—for example, the development of respect for divergent value systems and forms of political organization, the establishment of orderly processes of societal and political change (without external intervention), the rebuilding of respect for international law, the formation of effective peacekeeping systems, renewed dedication to protection of human rights, reduced military expenditures by all nations on a graduated basis, reduced sales of lethal weapons and associated technology to nations confronted with significant economic development difficulties, and the encouragement of the two nuclear superpowers to return to the processes of negotiation on military matters that served as the hallmark of the period of détente of the 1960s and 1970s.

As long as the process of negotiation exists, the hope remains that the United States and the Soviet Union will terminate their arms competition and actually reverse the process because negotiation on this critical issue is, at least from the theoretical perspective, the symbol of the ability of the two nations to coexist and, indeed, to get along with each other. As Christoph Bertram, the erstwhile director of the International Institute for Strategic Studies, has observed, arms control talks between the United States and the Soviet Union "[are] more than a symbol for Soviet-American détente: it *is* Soviet-American détente." Despite serious reservations about various approaches that have occurred during arms control negotiations of the past, he and other specialists have underscored the necessity of perpetuating the process of negotiation:

> A rupture in this process, while perhaps giving an unambiguous push towards the emergence of more promising methods of arms control, would only jeopardize the political base on which future negotiations depend.[9]

The pursuit of peace is one of the most laudable enterprises that statesmen can undertake. The record of accomplishments, in terms of treaties and conventions ratified since the formation of the United Nations, is prepossessing. However, the community of nations is no closer today to unearthing the means necessary to induce nations to have recourse to nonviolent means to resolve their differences. There are also no indications that nations possessing nuclear weapons are prepared to assume high risks through unilateral disarmament. Thus, the challenge today is to build on the past while fashioning new strategies for the prevention of nuclear war. Respect for international order and adherence to the rule of international law must become the primary preoccupation of all statesmen if a nuclear holocaust is to be averted. To these ends, the United Nations has a demonstrable role to play as well as the moral imperative to exercise leadership, especially where others flag or fail in efforts to pursue these ends.

In the chapters that follow, the views presented are those of the author, and should not be received as reflecting the official position of the U.S. government.

Table 1–1. Major Initiatives in Arms Control

Subject Matter	Date
Moratorium on Atmospheric Nuclear Testing	1958–1961
Antarctic (Military-Free-Zone) Treaty	1959
Hot-line Agreement (Revised 1971)	1963
Limited Nuclear Test Ban Treaty	1963
Outer Space Treaty	1967
Treaty for the Prohibition of Nuclear Weapons in Latin America	1967–1968
Nuclear Nonproliferation Treaty	1968

Table 1–1. *(continued)*

Subject Matter	Date
Seabed Arms Control Treaty	1971
Nuclear Accidents Pact (United States–Soviet Union	1972
Agreement on Prevention of High-Seas Incidents	1972
Biological Weapons Convention	1972
Strategic Arms Limitation Talks (SALT) Agreement I	1972
Anti-Ballistic Missile Treaty (amended 1974)	1972
Vladivostok Accords (guidelines for SALT II Agreement)	1974
Threshold Nuclear Test Ban Treaty (United States–Soviet Union)	1974
Peaceful Nuclear Explosions Treaty (United States–Soviet Union)	1976
Convention Banning Modification of the Environment	1977
SALT II Agreement	1979

NOTES

1. United Nations General Assembly resolution S-10/2, June 30, 1978, paragraph 18.
2. Michael Mandelbaum, *The Nuclear Future* (Ithaca, N.Y.: Cornell University Press, 1983), p. 24.
3. Ibid.
4. Results of the forum reported in *The New York Times*, December 9, 1983, p. A13.
5. The commission was superseded in January 1952, under General Assembly auspices, by the Disarmament Commission; in 1959, a Ten-Nation Disarmament Committee replaced the commission; the Eighteen-Nation Disarmament Committee was formed in 1962, which was enlarged in 1969 to twenty-six members and renamed the Conference of the Committee on Disarmament. This conference was further enlarged in 1975 to a total membership of thirty-one and, after the 1978 special session on disarmament, to forty, including all five nuclear powers. In 1984, its name was changed to the Conference on Disarmament.
6. Source of data in this paragraph and in the preceding list is U.S. Department of Defense, *Soviet Military Power* (Washington, D.C.: GPO, 1983) and independent research conclusions by the author.
7. United Nations General Assembly document A/S-12/PV-1, (1983), pp. 38–40.
8. Mandelbaum, *Nuclear Future*, pp. 76–77.
9. Christoph Bertram, ed., *The Future of Arms Control: Part I, Beyond Salt II,* Adelphi Papers (141) (London: International Institute for Strategic Studies, 1978), p. 3.

Chapter 2

Basic Means of Preventing Nuclear War

The delegates to the tenth special session of the General Assembly of the United Nations, June 30, 1978, expressed their alarm concerning the threat posed to the survival of humankind by the continuing nuclear weapons arms race. Noting that the disarmament decade declared by the United Nations in 1969 was coming to an end, the General Assembly observed that effective measures to produce a cessation of the race continued to elude the grasp of world statesmen. The Final Document, agreed to by consensus, also observed:

> There has not been either any real progress that might lead to the conclusion of a treaty on general and complete disarmament under effective international control. Furthermore, it has not been possible to free any amount, however modest, of the enormous resources, both material and human, that are wasted on the unproductive and spiralling arms race, and which should be made available for the purpose of economic and social development, especially since such a race "places great burden on both the developing and the developed countries."[1]

Because of the urgency of the threat, the delegates fashioned an impressive program to place those nations possessing nuclear weapons on the path to disarmament. Among the measures proposed were the following: (1) cessation of the qualitative improvement and development of nuclear weapons systems; (2) cessation of the production of all types of nuclear weapons and their means of delivery, as well as the production of fissionable material for weapons purposes; (3) a comprehensive, phased program for progressive and balanced reduction of stockpiles of nuclear weapons and their means of delivery, leading to their complete elimination at the earliest possible time; and (4) cessation of nuclear weapons testing by all states within the framework of an effective nuclear disarmament process. The delegates also encouraged the United States and the Soviet Union to conclude the SALT II negotiations as early as possible and then to proceed expeditiously to other arms reduction discussions.

Cognizant of the need to supplement the discussions of the two nuclear superpowers, delegates to the United Nations special session called for coordinated measures by the Secretary-General and his staff to encourage adherence to the Nonproliferation Treaty of 1968, encourage the establishment of nuclear-weapon-free zones in various regions, and study measures that might be taken to reduce military expenditures of all United Nations Member States. In addition, taking official note of the fact that the best efforts of the international community had not registered significant progress in these matters, the delegates recommended that additional machinery be organized to provide further impetus to United Nations efforts to encourage disarmament. In the words of the Final Document: "The most effective guarantee against the danger of nuclear war and the use of nuclear weapons is nuclear disarmament and the complete elimination of nuclear weapons."[2] Finally, the delegates took note of the need for nations with nuclear arsenals to take intermediate steps to diminish the likelihood of nuclear war. Among these was a pledge of no first use.

NONUSE OF NUCLEAR WEAPONS

The concept of the nonuse of nuclear weapons originated with the unlocking of the secrets of nuclear fission. In 1946, the United States, at a moment when it possessed a monopoly in knowledge and weaponry, adopted a nonuse approach by recommending to the United Nations and the community of nations that atomic weaponry be outlawed and the applications of nuclear physics be devoted entirely to peaceful pursuits. Embodied in the Baruch Plan, in 1946, the proposal was rejected by the Soviet Union. It has been resurrected on a number of occasions since, either in the form of an absolute ban against any use of nuclear weapons or a ban on first use, with varying degrees of support emanating from the five nations that currently maintain nuclear weapons inventories.

The United Nations special session on disarmament, convened in 1978, made specific reference in its Final Document to the matter. Indeed, paragraph 58 is of particular interest since it represents the only internationally agreed statement by the United Nations against the use of nuclear weapons. The document states that the most effective guarantee against nuclear war is the elimination of weapons associated with such war; pending achievement of this goal, the delegates agreed that nuclear-armed states have incurred a special responsibility to prevent the outbreak of nuclear war. It was further agreed (paragraph 58) that nuclear weapons states should consider various proposals designed to secure the avoidance of the use of nuclear weapons. The Final Document was reaffirmed at the second United Nations General Assembly special session on disarmament, which was convened in 1982.

Since the 1970s, the General Assembly has urged on various occasions that the nuclear-armed nations take formal and concrete action, in public pledges or treaty documents, against the use of nuclear weapons. However, reservations have been raised by Member States to such pledges or treaty commitments. First, representatives from several European nations and the United States have noted that the nonuse of nuclear weapons must be related to a total disarmament program—in brief, that pledges of nonrecourse have little tangible value unless confidence can be established that nuclear-armed nations are fully prepared to diminish the size of their arsenals, nuclear and nonnuclear, in a measured, verifiable, and balanced manner. Second, considerable disagreement exists as to what limitations on use, if any, should be agreed upon prior to or at the beginning of disarmament negotiations.

It is the official position of the member states of the North Atlantic Treaty Organization (NATO), formed in 1949 to provide an effective defense against the forces of the Soviet Union, that in the event of an unprovoked attack by the latter and, in extremis, NATO must be permitted to utilize all the resources at its disposal to defend the territory of member states. NATO has declared that the first recourse of member states, in such circumstances, would be to conventional armaments and conventional means of defense; however, should such measures not prove sufficient, NATO reserves the right to use nuclear weapons in its defense. NATO member states point out that, as members of the United Nations, they are pledged to support both the Charter and the principles of the world body relating to respect for the sovereignty and territorial integrity of all Member States, including the Soviet Union and all participants in the Warsaw Treaty Organization. The U.S. government, for its part, has underscored this position through official declarations that it would not use nuclear weapons or any other weapons except in defense of itself and its NATO allies against acts of aggression.

Flexible response is the touchstone of military strategy within NATO.

It embodies an approach that, according to the member states, is both prudent and balanced but one that also links all members to an approach that diminishes the prospect of war between the Warsaw Pact and the Atlantic Alliance. The basis for this belief resides, according to General Bernard Rogers, supreme allied commander in Europe (NATO), in the deterrent role played by the nuclear arsenals of member states in dissuading Warsaw Treaty Organization forces from attacking Western Europe. Other NATO officials have observed that recourse to no-first-use declarations would have a number of side effects unfavorable to United Nations advocates of total disarmament. For example, the Atlantic Alliance would be compelled, in consequence of no first use, to increase both its budgetary allocations and the manpower levels of its conventional forces to offset the perceived numerical and qualitative superiority of Warsaw Treaty Organization forces. In the final analysis, therefore, both treaty organizations would find themselves engaged in new weapons races at the conventional level – a development that would generate little confidence in protestations of support for disarmament. Moreover, such competition would inevitably lower the threshold of nuclear weapons use, according to leading West European defense specialists.

A more meaningful test of the capacity of the two treaty organizations to reach agreement on military and security issues is to be found in negotiations that, until recently, have been conducted in Geneva, Switzerland, and Vienna, Austria, relating to theater nuclear weapons and balanced reductions of conventional military forces. Of particular moment has been the subject of theater nuclear forces, a field in which both the U.S. government and the other member states of NATO had reason to hope that agreement could be reached. As is known, the Atlantic Alliance has been greatly disturbed over the past several years by the threat to the balance of forces in Europe posed by the decision of the Soviet Union to deploy large numbers of SS-20 nuclear missiles in the region. Since 1979, the Atlantic Alliance has pursued the twin goals of restoring the balance of intermediate-range nuclear weapons systems in Europe by either successful negotiations with the Soviet Union on the subject or, failing such agreement, to deploy offsetting U.S. missile systems. It was the hope of the U.S. government that a balance in theater forces could be established at the lowest possible level. The basis for this hope lay in the claim of the Soviet Union, periodically stated and reaffirmed since 1979, that a balance already existed. This claim was placed in doubt, despite Soviet statements, by the continued deployment of SS-20 batteries. The Soviet Union has refused to agree to a deployment moratorium on its part, while nevertheless insisting that the United States do so.

Illustrative of the Soviet approach, from 1979 until late 1983, is the fact that the number of Soviet SS-20 warheads aimed at Western European and East Asian targets increased from approximately 800 to in excess of 1,300.[3] During the same time frame, NATO did not introduce a single U.S. offsetting system. When, however, U.S. deployment of the Pershing II and ground-launched cruise missile systems commenced in late 1983 to re-establish a balance of theater forces, the Soviet Union summarily terminated its participation in the negotiations then in progress at Geneva, despite the urgent appeals by West European nations and the U.S. government that it exercise diplomatic restraint in the cause of international peace. The record of Soviet performance in this field leaves little room for confidence in the ultimate willingness of the Soviet Union to demonstrate flexibility in arms control negotiations. And, given the paucity of such evidence, there appears to be little disposition on the part of the member states of NATO to endorse no first use as an agreed posture of the defense alliance.

Two nuclear-armed nations have declared themselves in support of non-recourse, however. These are the People's Republic of China, which, after testing a nuclear weapon in 1964, stated that China would never be the first to use such weapons. Concomitantly, China suggested, as a measure preparatory to a world summit conference to discuss nuclear disarmament, that nuclear powers and near nuclear powers agree to ban first use; the proposal failed to secure support by the other nuclear nations. The Soviet Union, on June 15, 1982, pledged support for the general principle.

Some agreement, at least in principle if not in fact, appears to have been achieved concerning the question of first use against nonnuclear nations. During Soviet and U.S. discussions in relation to the Nonproliferation Treaty of 1968, efforts were made to provide negative assurances to nonnuclear nations. The United States and the Soviet Union unsuccessfully sought agreement on a common formula on a nonuse formulation. In what has been described as the Kosygin formula, the Soviet Union proposed assurances to parties that did not have nuclear weapons deployed on their territories. The United States rejected this proposal on the grounds that it discriminated against nonnuclear members of NATO. For its part, the U.S. government offered a modified formulation— namely, that nuclear weapons not be used against nonnuclear parties as long as these parties were not engaged in armed attack assisted by a nuclear weapon nation. This proposal failed to get Soviet acceptance.

The United States subsequently presented proposals that it characterized as positive security assurances. These were accepted, with modification, prior to the conclusion of negotiations on the Nonproliferation Treaty. The resulting document, while not a complete or universal nonuse undertaking, signified an implied understanding by the United States and the Soviet Union not to utilize nuclear weapons in any conflict situation involving a nonnuclear nation. In separate statements, identical in nature, the two governments agreed that aggression with nuclear weapons or the threat of such aggression against a nonnuclear party to the Nonproliferation Treaty "would create a qualitatively new situation" in which permanent United Nations Security Council members would "have to act immediately through the Security Council to counter such aggression or remove the threat of aggression."[4] The Security Council, in a separate resolution, endorsed without reservation this declaration of principle and intent. To have such effect, however, consensus must be obtained among the permanent members of the Security Council.

The prohibition of use of nuclear weapons is not confined to the nuclear nations solely. Regional organizations have the potential to establish nuclear-weapon-free zones, which, with suitable support from the nuclear nations, could provide a stable foundation for prevention of nuclear war in selected regions. The United Nations General Assembly has singled out several regions as potential candidates for establishment of nuclear-weapon-free zones—among them, the Middle East, South Asia, Africa, and Latin America. Only the latter has moved with vigor to establish such an arrangement. The effort was launched in 1962 with a proposal by the government of Brazil, followed by a joint declaration in 1963 by the presidents of Bolivia, Brazil, Chile, Ecuador, and Mexico, supporting the general principle of creation of a nuclear-weapon-free zone. The United Nations General Assembly welcomed the declaration, and after extensive negotiations among Latin American nations, the Treaty of Tlatelolco (Mexico) emerged in 1967. The treaty has entered into force for twenty-two Latin American and Caribbean nations but is not yet in effect for Argentina, Brazil, Chile, and Cuba.

The provisions of the Treaty of Tlatelolco can serve as a useful model for other geographic areas. In brief, the treaty (1) prohibits the testing of nuclear weapons in the territories of parties to the treaty and proceeds beyond the 1963 Limited Test Ban Treaty by prohibiting all forms of nuclear underground testing in the zone; (2) goes beyond the Nonproliferation Treaty of 1968 by prohibiting the receipt, storage, installation, or deployment of nuclear weapons in the territory of treaty parties—thus, effectively enjoining treaty adherents from permitting non-zone nations from using their territory for such purposes; (3) prohibits parties to the treaty from engaging in the testing, use, manufacture, or possession of nuclear weapons anywhere in the world; and (4) with respect to verification, requires the conclusion of agreements not only with the International Atomic Energy Agency but also with a regional control organization. Both agencies have the right to secure necessary information from treaty adherents regarding their nuclear programs and to conduct inspections in the territory of an adhering nation if such inspection is required to verify information supplied by said nation.

DÉTENTE, DETERRENCE, AND CRISIS MANAGEMENT

One of the paradoxes of the nuclear age is that, while nations perennially pledge to pursue peaceful purposes, they continue to arm themselves as if planning for war. While pledges, when encompassed in instruments such as resolutions of the United Nations, have the full force and effect of international law, the pledges are wholly dependent for execution and enforcement on the good faith of the parties involved. Good faith, or confidence in the willingness of nations armed with nuclear weapons to avoid their use in time of tension, is an important aspect of the efforts of the international community to diminish prospects for a nuclear holocaust. In the 1970s, a number of initiatives were launched, many under the auspices of the United Nations, to conclude agreements on the prevention of the use of nuclear weapons. The agreements, which represent a benchmark in international law, involved the United States and the Soviet Union, the Soviet Union and the United Kingdom, and the Soviet Union and France.

While all are of equal weight and merit, probably the most important of the agreements was that concluded between the United States and the Soviet Union during a conference of the leaders of the two nations in 1973. Referred to as the Agreement on the Prevention of Nuclear War, the parties declared in Article I that their intention is to eliminate the danger of nuclear war and of the use of nuclear weapons. To this end, they pledged that they would act to prevent the emergence of situations likely to engender an exacerbation of relations, to avoid military confrontation, and by all practicable means to take steps to preclude nuclear war between the United States and the Soviet Union or between each party and other nations.

An agreement was concluded between France and the Soviet Union in July 1976. Under the terms of their agreement, the two parties undertook to adopt measures to prevent accidental or unsanctioned use of nuclear weapons, to notify one another in the event of a nuclear accident, and to take such other steps to control crises as may be necessary. A comparable undertaking had been recorded between the Soviet Union and the United Kingdom in October 1970. The Soviet Union has concluded no comparable agreement with the People's Republic of China.

The clear purpose and intent of the parties to these agreements and

undertakings was, and continues to be, the avoidance of war as a result of misunderstanding, accident, or improper communication. The parties would undoubtedly accept the sober judgment of an eminent U.S. scholar, Professor Bernard Brodie (deceased), on the likely consequences of nuclear war:

> The cold war was to develop soon enough, in a mood of soberness deepened by knowledge that war, that is, what we have come to know as "general war," had entered a wholly new and hitherto unbelievable dimension of horror. In any new war between the superpowers, the terrible devastation of the two world wars would be at once immeasurably surpassed. Certainly the clarity of this realization was heightened and made more acute by the knowledge of what had happened in the two Japanese cities that had been struck, accounts of which were soon to be widely published with no want of detail. After more than a quarter of a century, they are still the only nuclear weapons to have been used in war, and their use has not made an iota more likely any future use. One would suspect that quite the contrary is the case.[5]

During the 1960s and 1970s, the primary emphasis placed by the United States and the Soviet Union in their bilateral relationship was on détente and crisis management. Progress was first made in reducing the risk of nuclear war by miscalculation, accident, or failure of communication. To accomplish this objective, inter alia, the establishment of rapid communication by direct link in case of emergency was agreed upon mutually. The so-called hot-line agreement was concluded between the United States and the Soviet Union in June 1963, updated by an accidents measures accord of 1971 and a subsequent hot-line modernization agreement. (The Soviet Union concluded comparable hot-line agreements with France and the United Kingdom in the same period.) Clearly, with the notable exception of the People's Republic of China, all the nuclear-armed nations were committed to a process of information interchange and accident notification that would diminish the chances of misperception and military alarm. In short, crisis management was viewed as an essential element in reducing the risk of nuclear war among the contracting nations.

The avoidance of nuclear war has been a responsibility that has weighed on every U.S. president from Harry S. Truman to Ronald Reagan. Each has advocated, although not always with the ultimate endorsement of the Soviet Union, a wide range of arms control agreements. The following initiatives warrant appreciation:

1. On September 23, 1960, in an address before the United Nations General Assembly, President Eisenhower proposed a series of steps

to be taken by Member States for the peaceful use of space, including: (1) agreement that celestial bodies should not be subject to national appropriation in the form of claims of sovereignty; (2) agreement that there be no warlike activities on celestial bodies; (3) agreement, subject to appropriate verification, that no nation "put into orbit or station in outer space weapons of mass destruction";[6] and (4) establishment of a program of international cooperation, under the auspices of the United Nations, for the peaceful uses of outer space.

2. On September 3, 1961, in response to resumption of nuclear tests in the atmosphere by the Soviet Union, President Kennedy and Prime Minister Macmillan (of the United Kingdom) urged the Soviet Union to join their nations in an immediate ban on atmospheric testing. The two Western leaders asserted that existing means of detection were sufficient to identify violations of an agreed ban. On September 9, the Soviet Union formally rejected the proposal. General Secretary Khrushchev averred that the Soviet Union would not agree to a test ban until general and complete disarmament had been achieved.

3. On September 25, 1961, President Kennedy presented to the United Nations General Assembly a proposal for general and complete disarmament, which called upon negotiating states to seek the widest possible area of agreement at the earliest possible date . . . and to continue their efforts without interruption until the whole program has been achieved.[7] The suggested program called for (1) immediate signing of a test ban treaty, independent of other ongoing disarmament negotiations; (2) ending production of nuclear weapons and preventing their transfer to nonnuclear nations; (3) preventing transfer of control of nuclear weapons to nonnuclear nations; (4) barring nuclear weapons in outer space; (5) gradually destroying existing nuclear weapons and transforming the use of nuclear materials to peaceful pursuits; (6) halting the testing and production of strategic nuclear delivery vehicles and gradually destroying existing inventories; and (7) earmarking national forces for call by the United Nations to perform peacekeeping duties, together with intensification of efforts to improve the operational effectiveness of United Nations peacekeeping machinery.

4. On April 18, 1962, the United States introduced a multistaged disarmament proposal for general and complete disarmament. Stage one provides for a three-step, 30 percent reduction of nuclear delivery vehicles and other major armaments, restrictions on arms production, reduction of U.S. and Soviet forces to 2.1 million, a nuclear production cutoff and transfer of fissionable material to

peaceful uses, an agreement not to transfer nuclear weapons to powers not possessing them, a test ban agreement, advance notification of missile launchings, reports on military spending, measures to reduce the risk of war, establishment of an international disarmament organization, and a study of measures to reduce and eliminate nuclear weapons stockpiles.

Stage two provided for a 50 percent cut of remaining delivery vehicles and armaments, a 50 percent reduction of U.S. and Soviet forces from first-stage levels, reduction of nuclear stocks, dismantling or conversion of certain bases, and further peacekeeping arrangements. Stage three provided for reduction of arms and forces to levels required for internal order, elimination of nuclear weapons from national arsenals, elimination of remaining bases (except those needed for retained forces), monitoring of military research, and strengthening of the United Nations peace force so that no state could challenge it. The first stage would take three years. No time limit is specified for the other stages. Ultimate decisions on timing and so forth would rest with the United Nations Security Council.

5. On January 21, 1964, the United States, at the eighteen-nation disarmament talks under the aegis of the United Nations, proposed that steps be taken to achieve nuclear weapons disarmament, including a verified freeze on deployment of nuclear weapons delivery vehicles; an agreement to halt production of fissionable materials for weapons; the closing of nuclear production facilities on a plant-by-plant basis under international supervision and verification; the establishment of observation posts against surprise attack; and the negotiation of agreements to prohibit transfer of nuclear weapons to nations not controlling them, placing under international safeguards and inspection all transfer of nuclear materials for peaceful purposes, and to ban all nuclear weapons tests (including underground tests) under effective international verification and control.

6. On March 18, 1969, President Nixon instructed the U.S. delegation to the eighteen-nation disarmament committee to seek discussion of a proposal for an international agreement prohibiting the placement of weapons of mass destruction on the seabed and ocean floor. The U.S. president noted that an agreement of this type would, like the Antarctic and outer space treaties, "prevent an arms race before it has a chance to start."[8]

7. On November 25, 1969, President Nixon declared that the United States unilaterally renounced first use of lethal or incapacitating chemical agents and weapons and unconditionally renounced all methods of biological warfare. Henceforth, the biological program of the United States would be confined to research strictly on clearly

and carefully defined measures of defense like immunization. The president further instructed the U.S. Department of Defense to prepare plans for the disposal of existing stocks of biological agents and weapons; these have since been prepared and the plans fully executed. Several months later, the United States unilaterally extended its ban on biological weapons to include toxins (i.e., chemical weapons produced through biological or microbic processes).

The 1970s witnessed other initiatives by the United States with respect to efforts to achieve general agreement on disarmament, both in the nuclear and conventional weapons fields. On the whole, these efforts were not well received initially by the leaders of the Soviet Union. The course on which the two governments finally agreed in their bilateral relations involved a mixture of political confidence building within the framework of détente together with crisis management and arms control, designated in the 1970s as SALT. The distinction between disarmament and arms control is of more than passing academic interest. Disarmament, by its nature, involves a degree of trust and confidence among the contracting parties that history suggests is difficult, if not impossible, to generate. The history of disarmament efforts since the beginning of the nineteenth century is replete with examples of high purpose and limited achievement. Arms control is a more acceptable generic form of international concord, as well as public policy within the United States.

The U.S. government and public at large are most anxious to avoid conflict situations likely to engender recourse to nuclear weapons. Both believe that disarmament actions could prove constructive. The actions taken by the Nixon Administration in the early 1970s in the area of biological weapons are instructive. However, the belief persists that the Soviet Union has failed to respond to initiatives by the United States during the 1970s to reduce international tensions within the framework of détente—as witnessed by the growth in Soviet arms sales to Third World regions, the dramatic increase in Soviet military expenditures and resultant growth in the Soviet nuclear arsenal, the deployment of SS-20 missiles, and the Soviet invasion of Afghanistan—as well as continued support by the Soviet Union for liberation movements and terrorist organizations whose main purpose has been to overthrow legitimately constituted governments. The latter are represented in the United Nations, whose Charter the Soviet Union is pledged to respect. Particularly pertinent from the U.S. perspective is Article 2, paragraph 4 of the Charter, which enjoins Member States "to refrain in their international relations from the threat or use of force." This injunction makes no distinction between threats involving nuclear weapons or threats to support armed insurgency or terrorist organizations.

The void that has widened between pledges by Member States to pursue peaceful means to achieve national goals and actual performance has produced a substantial challenge to the United Nations. The challenge is to develop initiatives that create an atmosphere of mutual trust and understanding, both of which are requisite for confidence building. By playing a constructive (initiative-taking) role, one that encourages an atmosphere of conciliation, the United Nations can enhance the respect for rules of right conduct and international order, as well as to narrow the void that has developed between its public pledges and actual performance by Member States.

From the date of its formation, the United Nations has defined arms control in comprehensive terms. The ultimate objective is to insure the maintenance of international peace. The Charter of the United Nations accords primary responsibility for the maintenance of international order and security to the Security Council, which is to act on behalf of the world community in dealing with international disputes and threats to the peace. National armaments and armed forces are to be subordinated to the Security Council, through agreements to be negotiated with that body, and all arms are to be subject to regulation. The term *regulation of armaments*, used in Article 26 of the Charter, is clearly intended to mean arms control. The failure of the permanent members of the Security Council to agree on a formula to meet the responsibilities assigned to that body for regulation, primarily due to the collapse of the alliance that had been fashioned during World War II and the resultant tensions produced by superpower disputes, has frustrated efforts to transform the United Nations into an effective worldwide security system.

In 1959, the General Assembly set general and complete disarmament as the goal to be pursued, a goal that was warmly endorsed by President Eisenhower and every U.S. president thereafter. In due course, the Soviet Union and the United States agreed to a set of principles as a basis for negotiations—within the United Nations and on a bilateral basis. These principles specifically related the problem of disarmament to the problem of preventing war. The goals of bilateral negotiations that were to be undertaken encompassed the following: (1) that disarmament would be general and complete and that war would no longer be an instrument for resolving international problems and (2) that disarmament would be accompanied by the establishment of reliable procedures for the peaceful settlement of disputes and effective arrangements for the maintenance of peace in accordance with the principles of the Charter of the United Nations. Almost immediately, however, the governments of the Soviet Union and the United States found themselves in disagreement on the standards to be utilized in beginning the process of nuclear weapons reduction. These differences over the balance between superpower weapons inventories diminished significantly the possibility of progress in any comprehensive approach to disarmament. During the following two decades, the United Nations, while endorsing a comprehensive approach, accepted the adoption of partial or collateral arms control measures.[9]

Even in the area of collateral measures, the United States and the Soviet Union failed to achieve overall agreement on an acceptable approach. The Soviet approach was broad in scope: the reduction of military budgets, a nonaggression pact between NATO and the Warsaw Treaty Organization, general prohibition of the use of nuclear weapons, the establishment of a nuclear-weapon-free zone for West and East Germany, the elimination of foreign military bases and the reduction in the number of armed forces in the two regional military organizations. The United States has tended to concentrate on narrower fields of limitation, utilizing the so-called building block approach to develop and strengthen confidence in mutual restraint. Thus, the United States and its allies have concentrated on three basic areas: (1) limitations on testing of nuclear weapons and deployment of defensive weapons systems, (2) limitations on the number of vehicles and warheads deployed or scheduled to be deployed within the rubric of strategic and intermediate-range nuclear weapons systems, and (3) reductions in the number of conventionally armed forces currently stationed in Europe. Soviet and U.S. accommodation has been achieved in several of these areas—notably, weapons testing, deployment of defensive systems, and limitations in the strategic weapons area. In addition, both nations have collaborated in efforts to secure adherence by all United Nations Member States to the Nonproliferation Treaty.

Progress registered to date in securing adherence to the Nonproliferation Treaty, including effective controls to insure compliance, has been impeded by the failure of the United States and the Soviet Union to meet their formal obligations under the terms of the Nonproliferation Treaty. These obligations include a pledge to cease and to reverse in the arms race and unilateral promises to submit their nonmilitary nuclear facilities to inspection and verification by the International Atomic Energy Agency.

Despite pledges to the contrary and the series of collateral agreements that have been concluded over the past fifteen years, the United States and the Soviet Union continue to be locked into a cycle of open-ended weapons competition in both the nuclear and conventional armaments fields. They do so in the belief that, given the absence of confidence in one another's pledges and stated intentions, national security can only be vouchsafed through a balance of nuclear forces. This balance has been enshrined in the concept of deterrence—a concept that is symbolized by the doctrine of mutual assured destruction or, appropriately, MAD. Simply stated, deterrence involves the capability to shape an adversary's calculations as to the likelihood of disastrous consequences if it commits an act of agression; the ability to deny an adversary any meaningful gain from aggression is felt to be the most effective means for dissuading a potential adversary from launching a military attack, with either conventional armaments or nuclear weapons. This requires that both the United States and the Soviet Union have the capacity to absorb an initial blow and to retaliate (second strike) with sufficient strength to destroy effectively both the societal foundations and the military capabilities of the adversary.

Deterrence means nuclear war prevention by means of an ever-present threat of far-reaching retaliation. Thus, in theory at least, deterrence is defensive in purpose and nature. Specialists argue that nuclear weapons lend themselves well to the concept of deterrence since they have no other purpose than the prevention of their own use. Moreover, according to such specialists, a nation that attempts to conquer an adversary through nuclear attack would render worthless the territory it attempted to occupy. The validity of the concept depends significantly, however, on a balance of terror, which entails the constant search for a means to insure that a potential adversary does not possess the capacity to strike a single disarming blow against one's arsenal. In brief, deterrence depends for its validity on an ability to establish clearly in the view of a potential adversary that a preemptive nuclear blow could not succeed in the sense of avoiding a devastating nuclear response.

The validity of the concept of deterrence in the avoidance of a nuclear war depends on several variables. The first involves a willingness on the part of the nuclear superpowers to commit themselves to parity in their respective arsenals and to avoid the initiation of programs to gain a qualitative or quantitative advantage. Deterrence, in terms of balance or equilibrium of opposing forces, will not serve as a stabilizing influence in international affairs if either of the superpowers attempts to secure a military advantage as a result of a technological breakthrough or a deployment program that appears threatening to the other.

Since deterrence is not an abstract notion subject to simple quantification, it depends in substantial measure on the perceptions of the leaders of the Soviet Union and the United States that security is not threatened by new military programs and development of technologies that record significant advantages. This was not the case as the 1970s came to a close. The U.S. public, as well as President Carter, became convinced that, despite efforts to broaden the basis for détente between the United States and the Soviet Union and the reductions that had taken place in U.S. military expenditure in the wake of the Viet Nam conflict, the

Soviet Union had not responded in kind. The growth in Soviet military capabilities was seen as threatening to the superpower military equilibrium. President Reagan pointed to the perceived challenge in an address before the Los Angeles World Affairs Council on March 31, 1983:

> Today, not only the peace but also the chances for real arms control depend on restoring the military balance. We know that the ideology of the Soviet leaders does not permit them to leave any Western weakness unprobed, any vacuum of power unfilled. . . . Yet, I believe the Soviets can be persuaded to reduce their arsenals—but only if they see it as absolutely necessary. Only if the Soviets recognize the West's determination to modernize its own military forces will they see an incentive to negotiate a verifiable agreement establishing equal, lower levels [of nuclear arms]. And, very simply, that is one of the main reasons why we must rebuild our defensive strength.[10]

The validity of the concept of deterrence also depends on a willingness to continue the processes of collateral arms control negotiations and to fashion an agreed formula for reductions in the nuclear inventory of the United States and the Soviet Union. In short, deterrence, confidence building, and arms control leading to elimination of whole classes of weapons systems need not be viewed as incompatible goals, given goodwill and trust on the part of the two nations most immediately concerned.

In a series of public initiatives, the government of the United States has sought not only to exercise restraint in the arms control field but also to seek reductions in the weapons inventories of the United States and the Soviet Union. Thus, on November 18, 1981, President Reagan proposed a zero option approach under which the Soviet Union would eliminate its previously deployed SS-20 intermediate-range ballistic missiles; in return, the United States would refrain from deployment of a new generation of intermediate-range missile systems that it had under development. The objective of the United States was to avoid the introduction of new generations of systems by both parties since the SS-20 and the Pershing II represented a qualitative advance that could only serve to threaten the military balance in Europe. The Soviet Union has unequivocally rejected this approach to arms control. Subsequently, the United States announced that it was prepared to embark on negotiations with the Soviet Union on strategic weapons, labeled START by the Reagan Administration, the acronym for Strategic Arms Reduction Talks. On May 9, 1982, President Reagan presented proposals for equal and verifiable reductions in the two nations' arsenals of long-range intercontinental ballistic missiles and submarine-launched intercontinental ballistic missiles. In October 1983, President Reagan, in instructions forwarded to the U.S. START delegation at Geneva, Switzerland, tabled the following formula for a build-down of strategic nuclear weapons arsenals:

A provision linking modernization to reductions, using variable ratios that identify how many existing nuclear warheads must be withdrawn as new warheads of various types are deployed;

A provision calling for a guaranteed annual percentage reduction— the United States proposed a minimum annual reduction of 5 percent;

A proposal to discuss the build-down of strategic bombers and limitations on air-launched cruise missiles that might be carried by bombers of the armed forces of the United States;

Negotiation of trade-offs in the forces of the two nations, taking into account Soviet advantages in missiles and U.S. advantages in bombers;

Establishment of a working group within the framework of the START negotiations to discuss the U.S. build-down proposals in the ensuing rounds of negotiations.

The Soviet ambassador attending the thirty-eighth session of the United Nations General Assembly, in a statement in the first committee, on the prevention of nuclear war, denigrated the aforementioned proposals by the U.S. government. His response, as well as the Soviet decision to postpone its participation in further START and intermediate-range negotiations at Geneva, represents a major setback to the processes of collateral negotiations and the cause of international peace.

A much ignored factor determining the validity of deterrence as a stabilizing, war prevention concept is found outside the realm of nuclear armaments and arms control negotiations. This factor relates to the much discussed and little applied dialectic of peaceful coexistence. Almost since the dawn of the nuclear age in 1945, competition between the Soviet Union and the United States has been a central fact of international life. Its roots are embedded in the sharply different value systems of the two national societies, the divergent goals they embrace, and the manner in which they view their roles in the community of nations. The Soviet Union is dedicated to revolutionary change in the world community, using instruments of violence where necessary; by contrast, the United States is committed to a community in which law, stability, and order abide. While recognizing the need for change in the international system, the leaders of the United States have repeatedly declared that such change should occur within the framework of peaceful negotiations and respect for the principles of international law.

A natural foundation for competition exists between the political beliefs and value systems of the Soviet Union and the United States. However, this competition need not lead to confrontation and the possibility of nuclear war if principles for peaceful accommodation can be established. The essential principles to guide the actions of nations should include the following: (1) respect for the sovereignty and territorial integrity of the Member States of the United Nations; (2) nonintervention in the internal affairs of Member States; (3) cessation of support for so-called liberation movements and terrorist groups that have as their primary objectives the overthrow of governments represented in the United Nations General Assembly; (4) support for efforts to strengthen international institutions having responsibility for mediation, arbitration, and conciliation; and (5) material support for the peacekeeping efforts of the United Nations, including the earmarking of forces to be made available at the request of the Secretary-General. The latter is of particular importance since it would serve to restore some measure of authority and responsibility to both the Secretary-General and the Security Council, as originally provided in the Charter of the United Nations, for the maintenance of international peace and stability.

Concomitantly, both superpowers must recognize that the concept of deterrence has little lasting value. Predicated on mutual suspicion and fears that aggressive designs can only be frustrated through preparedness for a catastrophic war, deterrence provides no satisfactory, long-term foundation for the prevention of war. Shared danger can only manufacture increased distrust on the part of the United States and the Soviet Union. The risks inherent in the present arms competition between the two superpowers are readily evident. Past treaties and solemn undertakings concluded between the United States and the Soviet Union, in combination with multilateral concords, have not precluded qualitative improvements in nuclear weapons systems, including innovations that could well upset the existing balance of deterrence capabilities.

There can be no doubt that, unless new impetus and fresh approaches to arms control are developed both within the framework of the United Nations and bilaterally by the superpowers, the present dynamic of competition will promote a nuclear overkill capacity that could prove threatening to both competitors. To slow this competition, new measures are imperative. These measures are identified and addressed in the next section and the chapters that follow. The likelihood of successful implementation depends, however, on the present texture of U.S. and Soviet relationships. In particular, the leaders of the two nations must develop an atmosphere of restraint. Clearly, the existing arms race is not likely to be terminated without mutual respect and the creation of conditions leading to mutual trust and confidence.

BUILDING MUTUAL TRUST AND CONFIDENCE

While all the wars waged since the conclusion of World War II have been local conflicts fought with conventional weapons, the focal point for international discussion in the arms control field has been overwhelmingly directed toward the reduction of tensions that could lead to nuclear war. Forty years after the beginning of the atomic age, however, there is little control by any international organization over the thousands of thermonuclear warheads possessed by the nuclear nations. There can be substantial comfort in the fact that no nuclear warhead has been launched in war against an adversary since Hiroshima and Nagasaki. The dangers posed by multiplying nuclear inventories is greater today than at the dawn of the atomic age.

The main responsibility for the prevention of nuclear war reposes with the United States and the Soviet Union. However, in recent years, a climate of suspicion and doubt has enshrouded the arms control negotiations of the two nations, and their diplomats and representatives have engaged in polemical exchanges in various international forums, including the United Nations. A number of initiatives need to be taken to reverse this trend and to re-establish a climate conducive to arms control. The first initiative relates to support for existing forums for negotiations. The Conference on Disarmament in Europe, which convened in Stockholm, Sweden, early in 1984, should serve as a useful forum for discussion of that region's basic security concerns. The Conference on Disarmament in Europe is of particular value, as noted by the U.S. representative in his statement to the first committee of the General Assembly on the prevention of nuclear war on November 3, 1983:

> The CDE [Conference on Disarmament in Europe] is of particular relevance to the cause of prevention of nuclear war, since the risks of nuclear conflict lie to a great extent in the tensions attendant on the existence of two powerful military alliance systems in Europe. The specific brief of the CDE is to consider proposals to "reduce the risk of military confrontation in Europe." While the CDE should not try to duplicate the work of other security negotiations, it can make a valuable contribution toward increasing military stability and negotiating confidence and security building measures to decrease the risk of war. Such measures could be designed to decrease the possibility of a surprise attack in Europe, to reduce the risk of war by accident or miscalculation and to improve channels of communication during times of crisis, thus increasing stability.[11]

Other opportunities by which to build for peace obtain today. Thus, the efforts of former Prime Minister Pierre Trudeau of Canada to create a third rail of confidence and communication on world peace warrant international support. The central purpose of the effort by the prime minister of Canada was to create a stable environment of "increased security for both East and West."[12] To do so, Mr. Trudeau sought to create a forum at which all five nuclear weapons states would attempt to negotiate limits on their nuclear arsenals, persuade nations to sign the Nonproliferation Treaty of 1968, seek a better balance of conventional forces in Europe, and open negotiations for banning the testing and deployment of high altitude antisatellite systems that endanger superpower command and control systems. The initiative by the Canadian premier, intended to suppress the nearly "instinctive fears, frustrations or ambitions which have so often been the reason for resorting to the use of force,"[13] also is a clear signal that a number of international statesmen are anxious to bring the United States and the Soviet Union into a constructive relationship of dialogue in the cause of peace.

While other leaders may seek to create new channels of communication for the prevention of nuclear war, the basic impetus for constructive effort must come from the United States and the Soviet Union. Here, too, concrete steps are imperative. For example, the United States and the Soviet Union must give urgent consideration to the reopening of negotiations intended to produce a comprehensive test ban treaty. Concomitantly, the START and so-called Euromissile negotiations must be resumed but probably within a different framework. Both should accept the reality that intermediate- and long-range nuclear systems, which have been the subject of separate negotiations might best be dealt with in a single context. By doing so, the intractable dilemma of the British and French nuclear systems, an artificial distinction if confined solely to the Euromissile talks, might be circumvented. Indeed, the dividing line between intermediate- and long-range nuclear delivery systems is academic at best given the growing accuracy and capabilities of the two systems.

Even should the two talks be merged, the United States and the Soviet Union must begin in all earnestness to address one another's most profound concerns. Thus, the Soviet Union must be aware of the mounting concern in the United States in the capabilities of the giant land-based SS-18 missile system; for its part, the United States must be prepared to acknowledge Soviet worries about the deployment of the so-called MX missile systems and the Trident II. During future talks, both nations' leaders must commit themselves to a regime of restraint if not absolute prohibition of research and development of outer space weapons systems, including antisatellite systems of the type that would have the potential to threaten one another's command and control networks. Equally meritorious would be agreement to confine efforts in other technological study fields—for example, deployment of enhanced radiation (neutron) weapons, new generations of bombers like the so-called stealth, and manufacture of particle beam defensive weapons systems. In brief, neither the United States nor the Soviet Union should proceed in future weapons development and deployment into fields that threaten to diminish one another's purely defensive capabilities or to provide an incentive for a preemptive nuclear blow. In addition, both nations need to acknowledge in their public policies that nuclear weapons, pending a final arms control agreement leading to disarmament, have no military value except to deter one's opponent from their use. No war-fighting strategy, weapons development plans, or military force structure should be formulated on anything more than such a posture.

In direct negotiations between the United States and the Soviet Union, a step-by-step approach should be encouraged by the United Nations and other interested parties. Confidence building requires a building-block approach to be successfully implemented. Deep-seated suspicion and inertia can be overcome if a tabula rosa approach is eschewed. At the same time, the United States, either unilaterally or in coordination with the Soviet Union, might wish to announce several new steps or measures to restore a climate propitious for successful completion of arms control negotiations. The following would undoubtedly have the desired effect.

Announce a Policy of No Immediate First Use

While ambiguity in deterrence strategy has a certain utility, the current increases in Euromissile deployments pose certain challenges to the validity of the strategy. It is obvious that in Europe, any act of aggression by the forces of the Warsaw Treaty Organization poses the threat of a widening of the conflict, including vertical escalation. Thus, no prudent leader within the Warsaw Pact would wish to assume risks that might produce wholly undesirable outcomes. Within NATO as well, there is growing recognition of the utility of recourse to conventional defense in the initial stages of East-West hostilities. This is subsumed within the agreed strategy of flexible response and can be built upon as a test of Soviet intentions during discussions in renewed START-Euromissile talks.

Renounce the Strategy of Launch-on-Warning

The primary danger of the launch-on-warning is that the United States or the Soviet Union could well be responding to a failure in their early warning communications system, a mechanical malfunction, or human error, as well as to a simple failure in communications. The assumption held by the two superpowers in their public positions is that they could not launch their weapons systems under conditions of preemptive attack. Such a posture cannot withstand close scrutiny. Given the 40,000 nuclear warheads possessed by the United States and the Soviet Union, a devastating retaliatory response under any forseeable future circumstance is virtually assured. Thus, the public policy of both powers should be to renounce a doctrine of launch-on-warning.

Renounce a Strategy of Decapitation Nuclear Blows

While neither nation has publicly admitted that it has formulated a strategy of command and control denial to the other in a nuclear war situation, research and development by both presents the possibility that such a strategy might be adopted. The Soviet Union, in particular, requires advance assurances on this score given Soviet concern about the technological advantages that the United States enjoys in the area of redundant command and control systems. Moreover, should failed communications or mechanical failure lead to misunderstanding of the intentions of a potential adversary, the continued availability of national command and control means should give pause to any future U.S. and Soviet leaders about the merits of launching a nuclear exchange.

Negotiate the Establishment of Weapons-Free Zones

The principal framework within Europe for security has been conventional force reductions within one forum—Mutual Balanced Force Reductions (MBFR)—and Euromissile talks in a second. Ignored throughout has been the feasibility of linkages of nuclear- and conventional-force-free zones. Thus, in the case of East and West Germany, a neutral zone of fifty kilometers might be established in which all conventional military forces and tactical nuclear weapons systems might be removed. An arrangement of verification, by on-site inspection teams representing nations such as Sweden, Switzerland, and Finland—or representatives designated by the Secretary-General of the United Nations Organization—would serve to instill confidence in such an agreement. In due course, comparable agreements might prove feasible, under United Nations auspices, for the Middle East, South Asia, and Africa.

Establish a Joint U.S. and Soviet Crisis Center

Several U.S. senators—notably, Sam Nunn and Henry Jackson—have proposed that the two superpowers establish a crisis control center linking the two national capitals. Staffed by competent civilian and military personnel, the proposed center would provide essential information to the leaders of both governments. In addition, the center would be a pathfinder for studying violations of international agreements and a critical point of information exchange between the two governments. The watchdog group would represent an institution that could serve as a hallmark of cooperation, verification, and confidence building between the two nations.

Reduce Tactical Nuclear Weapons

NATO has already announced that it intends to diminish substantially its stockpile of tactical nuclear weapons over the next several years. A comparable announcement of Warsaw Treaty Organization goals could well serve as the basis for a broadly based accord involving a significant diminution of tactical weapons deployed by both alliance organizations over the next several years. In due course, NATO and the Warsaw Treaty Organization might be prepared to negotiate a treaty calling for phased reductions of tactical nuclear weapons over a prescribed period of time.

Negotiate a Ban on Weapons in Space

Space clearly represents the new frontier of weapons competition between the nuclear weapons superpowers. This new frontier is both a challenge in terms of military advantage and a challenge in terms of arms control restraint. A significant litmus test of intentions would be an agreement of combined intentions to avoid competition in this new weapons frontier. A mixture of the measures, bilateral and unilateral, is not beyond the realm of consideration by the superpowers, including (1) establishment of a combined agency for the exploration of outer space, (2) negotiation of a reduction in the ratio of nuclear warheads to missile launchers, (3) establishment of criteria for second strike to insure that such strikes are under absolute control, (4) creation of agencies for joint U.S. and Soviet scientific research cooperation in nonmilitary fields and (5) delay deployments of U.S. Pershing II nuclear weapons delivery systems in Europe if the Soviet Union will agree to return to a broader negotiations framework involving both strategic and intermediate-range systems.

Beyond dispute is the capacity of the human mind to formulate a wide range of proposals for confidence building and for peace. What is not clear are the inclination and capacity of the leaders of the United States and the Soviet Union to accept the challenges and risks associated with the clearly desirable goals of nuclear war prevention and the establishment of standards for the maintenance of international order and peace.

In the latter context, both the superpowers and the regional and international organizations concerned with the maintenance of international peace must assume a wide burden of responsibility because the issues of nuclear war prevention and the peaceful resolution of disputes among Member States of the United Nations are inextricably linked, as is demonstrated in Chapter 3.

NOTES

1. Cited in Ralph M. Goldman, *Arms Control and Peacekeeping* (New York: Random House, 1982), p. 268.
2. Ibid., pp. 277–278.
3. U.S. Department of Defense, "Soviet Military Power" (Washington, D.C.: GPO, 1983) and author's own research study (unpublished).
4. U.S. State Department, *Security and Arms Control: The Search for a More Stable Peace* (Washington, D.C., 1984), pp. 33–34.
5. Bernard Brodie, *War and Politics* (New York: Macmillan, 1973), p. 56.
6. William H. Lewis, *In Search of Peace: American Initiatives* (Washington, D.C.: U.S. Information Agency, 1982), p. 9.
7. Ibid., p. 9.
8. Ibid., p. 11.
9. Some confusion has arisen as to the distinction that should be made between arms *control* and arms *limitation.* The former includes all actions, unilateral as well as multilateral, by which levels and kinds of armaments are regulated to reduce the likelihood of armed conflicts and the economic burdens of military programs. Arms limitation, in contrast, is a more narrowly defined area of control dealing primarily with weapons numbers and quality, rates of development and deployment, and means to be undertaken to supervise or verify compliance with international undertakings on the part of signatory nations to exercise due restraint.
10. Reported in *The New York Times,* April 1, 1983, p. 14.
11. U.S. State Department Bulletin (Washington, D.C., January 1984), pp. 26–27.
12. *The New York Times,* August 13, 1984. p. 5.
13. Ibid.

Chapter 3

Conventional Arms in a World of Conflict

In an address to the thirty-eighth session of the United Nations General Assembly on September 26, 1983, President Ronald Reagan pointed to the dangers that attend a community of nations unable to resolve disputes through peaceful means. Noting that the United Nations was founded in the wake of World War II to protect future generations from "the scourge of war" as well as to promote self-determination and "global prosperity," the president observed that the founders clearly wished to replace war as an international arbiter with a "world of civilized order." In his own words:

> Whatever challenges the world was bound to face, the founders intended this body to stand for certain values, even if they could not be enforced, and to condemn violence, even if it could not be stopped. This body was to speak with the voice of moral authority. That was to be its greatest power.[1]

In the years since its founding, the moral authority of the United Nations has proved insufficient to resolve disputes or to forestall eruptions of armed violence or violations of international codes of conduct or of terrorist acts. History, since 1945, unhappily demonstrates that governments and peoples represented in the United Nations have an enduring capacity for generating conflict. As President Reagan observed:

> [T]oday in Asia, Africa, Latin America, the Middle East, and the North
> Pacific, the weapons of war shatter the security of the peoples who live
> there, endanger the peace of neighbors, and create ever more arenas of
> confrontation among the great powers. During the past year alone, violent
> conflicts have occurred in the hills around Beirut, the deserts of Chad and
> the Western Sahara, in the mountains of El Salvador, the streets of Suri-
> name, the cities and countryside of Afghanistan, the borders of Kampuchea,
> and the battlefields of Iraq and Iran.[2]

Many nations and statesmen are persevering in efforts to establish
a securer world—one in which peace rather than war abides. The instinct
for survival is not a sufficient guarantor, however, that human suffering
will prove a significant inhibition against acts of violence. And the dread
danger in the years immediately ahead is that such violence will not
only erode the foundations of the United Nations but also lead ineluctably to an increase in the number of nations having advanced conventional and nuclear weapons. To the extent that the United States and
the Soviet Union become embroiled in these conflict situations, the cause
of peace is threatened with even more catastrophic consequences.

From the perspective of the U.S. government and many Americans concerned with the future of the community of nations, the issue of war
or peace cannot be reduced to colonialism, capitalism, communism, or
the nuclear arms race. The issue that threatens international security
is the disinclination of governments to seek remedial measures other
than armed conflict to resolve differences. As a result, the threat of catastrophic conflict mounts. Nations today are not prepared to reduce their
military expenditures; of even greater criticality, they refuse to enter
into constructive discussions to diminish the burgeoning trade in conventional armaments that has developed as a growth industry since the
1960s.

Many developing nations have expressed reservations to international
restraints on the grounds that the superpowers continue to amass
arsenals of nuclear and conventional weapons, which activity serves as
the principal threat to world peace. The proposition is often put that
regimes of restraint must first begin with the superpowers, followed by
other nuclear-weapons-bearing nations. Once such self-control is established among the major powers, the developing nations would be under
moral obligation and general imperative to follow their example. The
validity of this contention is to be found in the fact that superpower disagreements and competition operate on a global scale, thus compound-
ing the security concerns of developing nations. The mounting number
of Third World conflicts and the recourse of the major powers to proxy
or surrogate wars threaten to lead the latter into direct confrontation—

hence, the danger of linkages between conventional and nuclear wars is evident.

REDUCTION OF CONFLICT

The Secretary-General of the United Nations, Javier Pérez de Cuéllar, in his annual address to the General Assembly in September 1983, observed that efforts to build an international system designed to provide "peace, security, stability, and justice for all" has experienced severe erosion. In his words:

> We are at present in a period when the value of multilateral diplomacy is being questioned and international institutions are not functioning as they were intended to function. . . . This applies to the United Nations and, in different degree, to regional organizations and to many international agencies and groupings. Nor is it evident that bilateral diplomacy or unilateral efforts are, in most cases, filling the gap.[3]

Conflict and recourse to armed forces to resolve disputes in the Third World have proliferated dangerously over the past decade. The causes are multiple, ranging from failure of governments to meet minimal needs of diverse populations, to irredentism, ideological divergences, and personal animosities. In addition, recessionary economic forces in the global community have added to the pressures and causes of instability. Many Third World nations currently face a staggering array of economic difficulties, involving debt servicing, adverse balances of trade, diminished productivity, mounting population pressures, massive underemployment of available laborpower, and an assortment of related ills.

During the period 1977 through 1980, the United States followed a policy of unilateral restraint in its transfer of conventional weapons abroad. Under the policy announced by President Carter in May 1977, arms transfers were to be viewed as an exceptional instrument of foreign policy, one whose use was to be carefully and rigorously constrained. Special controls were subsequently placed on U.S. arms transfers to Third World nations, including a declining annual dollar ceiling on transactions. The application of these restraints was accompanied by efforts on the part of the U.S. government to obtain the cooperation of the Soviet Union and Western European nations to reduce the level of international arms trade. These efforts, for a wide variety of reasons, registered few results and were ultimately abandoned late in 1980. Of particular interest, the United States and the Soviet Union conducted four rounds of bilateral negotiations (designated Conventional Arms Transfers talks) between December 1977 and December 1978. These talks were intended to establish a regime of restraint on the part of the two nations. With the invasion of Afghanistan by Soviet forces in December 1979, the talks were terminated, as were discussions being conducted concurrently on establishing the Indian Ocean as a zone free of superpower naval (military) presence.

In practical terms, there is little in the experience of the United States to suggest that a unilateral policy of arms export restraint on its part would be viewed by other arms-producing nations as a model to be followed. Available data indicate that the latter would regard a self-denying ordinance on the part of the United States as a unique opportunity to enter new markets, acquire new customers, and develop other commercial advantages. Statistical information compiled by the United States Arms Control and Disarmament Agency substantiates this conclusion.[4] Indeed, the acceleration of the arms trade to Third World nations has reached alarming proportions in recent years. The former director of the Arms Control and Disarmament Agency, Mr. Eugene V. Rostow, was sufficiently disturbed to observe, in March 1982, that the growth of military expenditures and arms acquisitions worldwide is:

> [A] fever chart, recording the disintegration of world public order, and the consequent spread of anarchy, fear, and panic in many parts of the world. As a result, the arms industry has become the leading growth industry in the world. The statistics in this report reveal that large and small countries on every continent have been scouring the world for arms, buying from governments or from private merchants in a desperate and often futile effort to guarantee their security.[5]

Today there is no more pressing requirement for world leaders and statesmen than to moderate and resolve regional conflicts that threaten global economic and political stability. Nations in general, and their leaders in particular, have an obligation to exercise restraint in areas of tension, to negotiate disputes and settle them peacefully, and to strengthen the peacemaking capabilities of the United Nations and regional organizations. To these ends the United States and the Soviet Union, together with other arms-producing nations, should accord urgent consideration to the initiation of arms control talks with a view to accomplishing the following:

Establishment of a code of restraint on future transfers of sophisticated weaponry to Third World regions, including agreement on prohibited items and producer ceilings on cash volume of sales for each region;

Formation of a reporting system whereby each party to the code provides data, on an annual basis, dealing with past and planned transfer agreements by region;
Agreement to submit disputes that arise to binding arbitration.

A concomitant of this approach should be a concerted effort by regional organizations, supported by the United Nations, to secure agreement on the part of the Soviet Union and the United States to avoid projection of their disagreements into Third World regions.

THE CORRELATION OF CONVENTIONAL AND NUCLEAR WAR

The U.S. perception of Soviet intentions and capabilities as they relate to conflicts in the Third World is shaped by public statements by Soviet leaders, as well as by Soviet behavior in the community of nations. From the inception of the Soviet regime, communist publicists have identified what they contend is a unique relationship between the USSR and those regions now known as the Third World. Lenin argued that the class struggle would be intensified in the latter area due to Western imperialism and colonial expansion, the result being a natural alliance between those peoples who have experienced colonial domination and the leadership of the Soviet Union. The Communist party of the Soviet Union is accorded the honor of serving as the cutting edge of this revolutionary process. The primary geographic zone for producing the anticipated correlation of historical forces—designated the national liberation zone—was initially viewed as extending from North Africa, bordering on the strategically vital Mediterranean basin through the Horn of Africa and the Middle East, into countries of South Asia that are in close geographic proximity to the Soviet Union. Within these areas, the Soviet Union fashioned a dual-track approach involving the establishment of diplomatic relations with governments of newly independent nations while encouraging local movements and groups in the promotion of revolutionary violence. According to a report prepared by the U.S. Congressional Reference Service:

> From the Soviet view, this national liberation zone is supremely important . . . because of the strategic raw materials and human resources that lie within it, the communications and commercial lifelines that intersect it, and the geographic reality that it is adjacent to the USSR and the socialist bloc. Within this zone most local conflicts of the postwar era *had* been fought—and are still being fought; and within it also are the leading contingents, the vanguards . . . of the national liberation struggle.[6]

During the 1970s, the geographic zone was expanded to include southern Africa, the outer periphery of the Saudi Arabian peninsula, and Central and South America. The expansion of this zone of competition caught many U.S. policymakers and foreign affairs specialists by surprise since the decade was expected to be one of mutual accommodation and reduction of superpower tensions, within the framework of a much heralded policy of superpower détente.

In reality, there should have been little occasion for U.S. expectation of a basic alteration in Soviet policy or strategy. Chairman Brezhnev made this evident in 1973, when he stated that while the United States and the Soviet Union might achieve a measure of accommodation, a state of permanent competition and conflict would prevail between the two nations. "Let me remind you," he declared, "the revolution, the class struggle, and Marxism-Leninism are fighting to ensure favorable international conditions for advancing the cause of social progress." To place themselves in the vanguard of such progress, the Soviet leader opined, meant that the Soviet Union would "continue support for the worldwide revolutionary process," which is part of the "worldwide transition from capitalism to socialism."[7] This perspective was consistent with the view that the correlation of historical forces was beginning to favor Soviet policies and objectives in the Third World. Statements by leading Soviet officials tended to underscore this assessment. Thus, Marshal Sokolovsky, in the officially sanctioned treatise, *Military Strategy*, wrote the following passage:

> One of the most important factors of today is the national-liberation revolutions which are destroying the colonial system of imperialism. The international revolutionary movement of the working class is expanding. . . .
>
> National liberation wars, civil wars and other popular wars [are] aimed at the repulsion of aggressive predatory attacks of the imperialists, at the fight for freedom and independence. Such wars are the opposite of imperialist wars. . . .
>
> The CPSU and all Soviet people . . . consider it our duty to support the sacred struggle of oppressed peoples and their just wars of liberation against imperialism. This duty the Soviet Union discharges consistently and steadily by helping the peoples in their struggle with imperialism not only ideologically and politically, but materially as well.[8]

Since the beginning of the 1970s, the views presented by Marshal Sokolovsky have been endorsed and sanctioned by the leadership of the Soviet Union. Authoritative statements by senior officials confirm that the Soviet Union has as a principal objective the disruption of Western relations with Third World nations, support for movements intended to overthrow bourgeois regimes, and attacks on capitalist centers of commerce and economic exchange with Third World nations.

It is an article of messianic faith in the leading circles of the Soviet Union that the Soviet Union has a historic mission to perform, whether or not Third World governments are disposed to accept the legitimacy of this mission or the peoples involved are willing to accept the sacrifices that are entailed. For the United States, such missionary zeal is treated with considerable reserve. Also treated with reserve are clear indications of contradiction and incoherence in Soviet policies and actions in the Third World. Thus, the United States views the injection of Soviet troops into Afghanistan as an example of blatant intervention in the affairs of a neighbor and is sympathetic to the efforts of Afghan citizens to liberate their country from such intervention. Similarly, the United States finds itself baffled by the intervention of the military forces of Viet Nam in neighboring Kampuchea and the willingness of its Soviet ally to provide military assistance to the offending party. The free world can only applaud the efforts of Kampuchean nationalists to liberate their country from the domination of Viet Nam. Other contradictions in Soviet behavior in the Third World abound. For example, the Soviet Union has become the principal arms supplier to Libya, whose leader, Muammar Qadaffi, is constantly and consistently accused of acts of intervention in the affairs of other sovereign states. Such acts hardly constitute liberation, even within the ideological lexicon of the Soviet Union.

Since the 1960s, each U.S. president has attempted to devise appropriate policies to diminish the likelihood of nuclear war or armed confrontation between the conventional forces of the United States and the Soviet Union that could lead to nuclear war. During the period of détente, the United States engaged in an earnest search for mutual accommodation – a formula that would ensure that the vital interests of the two nations would be safeguarded while concomitantly producing agreement on means to be adopted for avoiding crisis situations that might impel the two nations toward armed confrontation. In the process, it was hoped that accommodation might produce an agreed brokership of local conflicts that threaten the broader global equilibrium. Preventive and ameliorative diplomacy were the hallmarks of this approach. However, two developments undermined the détente of the 1970s: (1) the Soviet Union's persistence in seeking an advantageous military balance that exceeded most U.S. expectations of parity and (2) persistence by the Soviet Union in efforts to exploit situations of instability and disorder in the Third World.

The consequence of these frustrated hopes and expectations has been the adoption of a two-track approach by the United States in the 1980s. The first track involves continuation of efforts to reach agreement on arms control and disarmament; the second, which is regarded as both prudent and sound, based on past experience, has been to emphasize the need to build military forces capable of meeting crises and contingencies that threaten the vital interests of the United States. The intellectual underpinnings of the second track reposes in the theory of escalation dominance—to wit, the Soviet Union has expended increased financial resources on all sectors of its military establishment and those of its surrogates in order to dictate the location, timing, and level at which conflicts might be initiated to the advantage of the Soviet Union. This has engendered a countervailing strategy:

> The argument goes that the United States must match the Soviet Union at each level of force, or at least at each important level. If the United States is inferior at any of them, the Soviet Union can gain an advantage by attacking, or threatening to attack, at any level. The United States would then have to choose between accepting defeat and moving to the next highest rung on the ladder—"escalating" the conflict. There would, however, be strong inhibitions against escalation, for it might get out of control and propel both sides to the very top of the ladder and a mutually disastrous nuclear exchange.[9]

The fear exists in some circles that Soviet dominance in the strategic nuclear field would inevitably lead to coercive diplomacy on the part of the Soviet Union in Third World areas. Hence, the United States is compelled to act against Soviet efforts to achieve escalation dominance. Force modernization in the military realm involves denial of Soviet dominance by maintaining strategic nuclear parity with the Soviet Union while fashioning versatile conventional forces capable of engaging in combat at all foreseeable levels of conflict. Designated a strategy of flexible response by the U.S. government, it is justified as both a means of denying clear military superiority to the Soviet Union while serving as a means of confining future conflict situations to the conventional force level.

THE NEED FOR DIALOGUE

At the conclusion of World War II, the United States adopted a global foreign policy that stressed the need for peaceful resolution of international disputes. With expectations of a peaceful world, the United States looked initially to the United Nations to play a primary role. For a variety of reasons, the capacity of the United Nations to mute conflicts and to reduce the incidence of international violence has diminished.

In due course, U.S. involvement in global security issues grew because of U.S. perceptions that an international struggle for power and influence was being unleashed by the Soviet Union. Despite its performance, the United States continued to hope that a basis for mutual respect and accommodation might be found. The search for an acceptable formula continues to this day.

Confidence-building measures are an integral part of the foreign policy of the United States, given the U.S. effort to achieve greater international security and stability. These measures, as conceived by several generations of U.S. leaders, are designed to reduce the possibility of an accidental confrontation between the United States and the Soviet Union, miscalculation by either party, or a failure of communication. They have other purposes as well—namely, to diminish the likelihood of unanticipated (surprise) military attack by a potential adversary and to institutionalize procedures for the control of unfolding crisis situations. With respect to the Soviet Union, several agreements have been concluded to diminish the risks of war, including a hot-line agreement establishing direct communications links between the two national capitals, the 1971 Accidents Measures Agreement intended to prevent accidental nuclear war, and the 1972 Incidents at Sea Agreement, which is intended to prohibit acts at sea that also could increase the risk of war.

In addition, under the terms of the 1975 Final Act of the Conference on Security and Cooperation in Europe—the Helsinki Accords—the United States, Canada, and thirty-three European NATO, neutral, and Warsaw Pact nations agreed to a series of multilateral confidence-building measures. The most significant of these provides for prior notification of large-scale military maneuvers to reduce the risk of conflict arising through misperception or misinterpretation. Prior notification, provision of information, and attempts to establish a basis for agreement on on-site inspection, are an additional part of the NATO–Warsaw Treaty Organization negotiating process that has been in progress on mutual and balanced force reductions since 1973. In 1983, the United States also initiated negotiations with the Soviet Union to add a high-speed facsimile capability to the existing hot-line agreement, to establish a joint military communications link between the two nations, and to enhance existing channels of diplomatic communication. The United States has even proposed an agreement that would be open to all nations to facilitate consultations concerning unexplained nuclear accidents.

These recommendations and proposals have broad application beyond the geographic confines of the European continent. In recognition of this fact, the United States is actively supporting the United Nations Disarmament Commission in exploring regional approaches to enhance confidence building and crisis management. The United Nations clearly has the capacity to assume a role of leadership in sponsoring conferences dedicated to the principles of crisis management by regional organizations, including consideration of arms control and disarmament goals that might be adopted, strengthening of regional capabilities for peaceful resolutions of local disputes, collective peacekeeping planning, and creating emergency communications links between nations holding membership in regional organizations. Should such steps be undertaken under the auspices of the United Nations, they would constitute a signal contribution to the cause of peace.

The ultimate success or failure of these measures would depend significantly, however, on the future texture of U.S.-Soviet relations. Both nations have the capacity to enlist in the cause of peace, without precondition or reservation. For the leaders of the two superpowers to accede on terms satisfactory to their national constituencies would depend substantially on their willingness to accept risks in the cause of peace. The record to date provides little room for optimism. Former President Jimmy Carter, during the initial stages of his presidency, noting the cooperative and competitive aspects of détente, advocated making the Soviet-U.S. relationship broader and more reciprocal. Mr. Carter accorded high priority to the necessity for reducing the nuclear arsenals of the superpowers. As a result, he adopted policies that emphasized arms reductions and respect for human rights under the terms of the Helsinki Accords and abjured U.S. intervention in the internal affairs of other nations. The expectation on the part of the U.S. government in 1977 was that the Soviet Union would signal a willingness to adopt reciprocal policies. The invasion of Afghanistan late in 1979 spelled the collapse of these expectations and led President Carter to embark on a program of military force improvement, a program that has been enlarged by his successor, President Reagan.

In 1984, the climate of relations between the United States and the Soviet Union deteriorated perceptibly, threatening a renewed round of political, ideological, and military competition. The situation has reached a juncture where the Member States of the United Nations have uniformly expressed their dismay and widening concern. Such expressions, while salutary, are not likely to provide a basis for renewed dialogue between the leaders of the two superpowers. More forthright action is required, action that is not beyond the capacity of the United Nations to sponsor. In particular, the Secretary-General might wish to consider the role of international broker, with the endorsement of the General Assembly. His responsibility, inter alia, would be to urge the appointment of special envoys by the United States and the Soviet Union to meet under his chairmanship for the purpose of launching a global review of their existing relationship, including an identification of outstanding issues that divide the two nations and an adoption of confidence-building measures to reduce tensions. The ultimate goal of such discussions should be the scheduling of a series of meetings between the heads of state of the United States and the Soviet Union to codify steps that might be taken both to diminish the prospects of conflict and to strengthen the role of the United Nations to meet its responsibilities, as outlined under the charter, for collective security.

NOTES

1. President Ronald Reagan, "Renewing the U.S. Commitment to Peace," Address given in New York before the United Nations General Assembly, September 26, 1983. Published by the U.S. Department of State, no. 511, Washington, D.C.
2. Ibid.
3. Reported in the Washington Post, September 23, 1983, p. 22.
4. See "World Military Expenditures and Arms Transfers, 1970–79" (Washington, D.C.: U.S. Arms Control and Disarmament Agency, March 1982).
5. Ibid., p. II.
6. U.S. Congress, House, Committee on Foreign Affairs, *Soviet Policy and United States Response in the Third World,* 97th Cong., 1st sess., 1981, pp. 35–36.
7. Cited in Stephen S. Kaplan, *Diplomacy of Power* (Washington, D.C., Brookings, 1981), p. 172.
8. V. D. Sokolovsky, *Soviet Military Strategy,* edited and translated by Harriet Fast Scott (New York: Crane, Russak and Co., 1975), pp. 180–184.
9. Michael Mandelbaum, *The Nuclear Future* (London: Cornell University Press, 1983), p. 56.

Chapter 4

The Nonproliferation of Nuclear Weapons

Preventing the spread of nuclear weapons has been a major goal of the overwhelming majority of Member States of the United Nations. In their effort to establish a regime of restraint, virtually all have seen a linkage between nuclear competition and the threat of proliferation of nuclear weapons. Cooperation also has its perils. While accepting the utility of developing nuclear power plants for peaceful purposes, the fear has developed since the dawn of the atomic age that the acquisition of this technology for avowedly peaceful purposes could lead some Member States to embark on nuclear weapons development programs. The consequences of such actions would be threatening in the extreme. The first special session of the United Nations General Assembly devoted to disarmament took particular cognizance of this threat: The General Assembly, in the Final Document of the first special session on disarmament, observed: "It is imperative, as an integral effort to halt and reverse the arms race, to prevent the proliferation of nuclear weapons" (paragraph 65).[1] Recognition of this imperative led the United States and many other nations to accept the necessity of controlling the dissemination of nuclear technology as a means of preventing, to the extent possible, the spread of nuclear weapons. Halting the spread of nuclear weapons while guiding nuclear development toward peaceful ends has been a central policy objective of every U.S. administration since 1945.

Within the community of nations, two distinct schools of thought have evolved on the subject of nuclear weapons proliferation. One school perceives the likelihood of proliferation as being inextricably linked to the spread of nuclear technological capabilities. It contends that the dissemination of nuclear materials, equipment, and technical competence generates a high risk of diversion to weapons development. Predicated on this assumption, the exponents contend that the only prudent policy to be adopted by the United Nations and those Member States possessing essential materials and technology is to limit the export of nuclear materials, equipment, and technology. Denial, both in principle and in practice, is the only feasible safeguard against proliferation. The second school perceives the issue of proliferation in political terms. It holds that efforts to restrict or otherwise impede the spread of technology, as a sole strategy, are not likely to diminish the likelihood of proliferation. According to this school, the only realistic approach for Member States is to broaden efforts at international cooperation and reliable nuclear supply (with effective safeguards) in order to reduce pressures for nuclear power independence. This approach would be coupled with intensification of efforts to secure adherence to the Nonproliferation Treaty of 1968, including strict compliance with its safeguard provisions, and renewed efforts to reduce international tensions.

The United States typically subscribes to the approaches recommended by the second school. Since 1945, the United States has been willing to share its achievements in the civil uses of nuclear energy in exchange for commitments confining the application of U.S. nuclear technology to peaceful purposes. On July 16, 1981, President Ronald Reagan outlined his approach to this form of cooperation. He officially declared that the United States will:

Seek to prevent the spread of nuclear explosives to additional countries as a fundamental national security and foreign policy objective;

Strive to reduce the motivation for acquiring nuclear explosives by improving regional and global stability and promoting understanding of the legitimate security concerns of other states;

Continue to support adherence to the Treaty on the Nonproliferation of Nuclear Weapons and the Treaty for the Prohibition of Nuclear Weapons in Latin America (Treaty of Tlatelolco) by countries that have not adhered to these treaties;

View a violation of these treaties or an international safeguards agreement as having profound consequences for international order and bilateral relations with the United States;

Strongly support and work with other nations to strengthen the International Atomic Energy Agency and its safeguards system;

Collaborate with other nations to combat the risks of proliferation;

Continue to inhibit the transfer of sensitive materials, equipment, and technology, particularly where the danger of proliferation exists, and to seek agreements accepting International Atomic Energy Agency safeguards in all nuclear activities in nonnuclear weapons states as a condition for any nuclear supply agreement with the U.S. government.[2]

Civilian use of nuclear energy has been a central purpose of U.S. policy since 1945. Former President Eisenhower, for example, pledged his support before the United Nations in December 1953 for an international atoms-for-peace program. The U.S. president offered Member States assistance in developing nuclear energy in return for pledges to use nuclear technology solely for peaceful purposes. This assistance took the form of research reactors, hardware, technology, and training for thousands of engineers and scientists. Subsequently, the Atomic Energy Act of 1954 by the U.S. Congress eliminated the U.S. government's monopoly on nuclear technology and opened the way for the domestic use of nuclear energy (generating electricity and industrial and medical application) by private firms under a formal licensing procedure.

Within the United Nations, the United States continued to urge the establishment of an international agency to deal with atomic energy matters. Using the atoms-for-peace proposal as the basis for discussion, the United States played a seminal role in founding the International Atomic Energy Agency in 1957. The agency had two basic purposes: (1) to promote the peaceful application and uses of atomic energy and (2) to establish and administer safeguards to insure that these technologies were not used for military purposes. The United States regularly contributes about one-third of the agency's operating budget through voluntary and assessed contributions.

On the technological level, the United States has continued to search for means to ensure compliance with the Nonproliferation Treaty and to safeguard in its own bilateral programs against proliferation. Significant progress has been made in the U.S. effort to guard against proliferation— for example, reduced enrichment for fuels for test and research reactors. It is the expectation of the United States that, when taken together with the efforts of other collaborating governments, these efforts will help to diminish and ultimately eliminate traffic in highly enriched uranium, while still permitting nations to meet their research and scientific program objectives. The United States has also adopted a prudent plutonium policy. Believing that the potential risks of reprocessing and use of plutonium as a fuel must be recognized, while also recognizing that legitimate research requirements can arise, the United States has launched collaborative ventures with interested parties to refine and elaborate existing safeguards for the use of plutonium in their peaceful energy programs.

Competition in the civil sector has added a new, complicating factor to international safeguard efforts. Among industrialized nations, there has been a considerable growth in projected energy demand. Competitive pressures in these countries and in less developed countries have created markets in which safeguards may not always and everywhere be respected. As one U.S. official has observed:

> The prospective emergence of new suppliers on the scene adds even greater urgency to efforts to preserve and strengthen the agreed rules of nuclear trade. If there is disharmony and controversy among the major nuclear suppliers on conditions for nuclear export, new suppliers inevitably will be tempted to use nonproliferation conditions as a bargaining factor in their pursuit of sales. If they see their role models performing in this way, what else can we reasonably expect? By contrast, agreement now among suppliers on sound guidelines will make it easier to urge new suppliers to follow those agreed and sensible export practices in the future.[3]

Various strategies have been proposed for strengthening safeguards, including a new international convention involving effective controls, inspections to be replaced by continuous on-site monitors, and censuring of nations that refuse to comply with existing safeguard standards. On the diplomatic level, major producer nations have been urged to establish a commonly agreed code of conduct. All these proposals have merit, but they are exceedingly difficult to adopt. Supplier nations have different standards for evaluating requests for nuclear technology, fuel, and facilities, and many are loathe to surrender these standards to a universally applied code. They prefer to address the subject on a case-by-case basis. Nonsupplier nations also are resistant to the imposition of stricter, more enforceable safeguards. In particular, many would regard proposals for on-site monitors as an infringement of their national sovereignty. In short, most strategies propounded to prevent the spread of nuclear weapons capability, to react to undesirable activities by a non-nuclear state, or to preempt such activity through a policy of resource denials have certain inherent limitations. As a result, in its deliberations the United Nations has concluded, inter alia, that nonproliferation preventive diplomacy should stress elimination of those factors and conditions that are likely to impel Member States to turn toward the acquisition of nuclear weapons. In the interim, continuation of efforts to secure adherence to both the Nonproliferation Treaty and its safeguard provisions are a matter of the highest priority to the United Nations.

Nuclear weapons development has two basic dimensions—the vertical, which involves expansion of inventories and capabilities on the part of nations that already possess nuclear weapons, and the horizontal, which is taken to mean expansion in the membership of the nuclear weapons "club." Reflecting shared and growing concern about the danger of nuclear proliferation, the government of Ireland recommended before the United Nations in 1961 that an international agreement be fashioned to halt the spread of nuclear weapons. With the support of both the United States and the Soviet Union, this suggestion evolved into the Nuclear Nonproliferation Treaty, which was completed in 1968 and came into force in 1970. By late 1985, the treaty had been ratified by 130 countries, including the Soviet Union, the United States, and the United Kingdom. The significance of the adherence of the weapons states reposes in their pledge to eschew aid to nonnuclear weapons states wishing to develop nuclear weapons or explosives. The nonnuclear weapons states that have ratified the treaty, in turn, renounce the right to manufacture or otherwise acquire nuclear weapons. Of equal importance, the latter also pledge to place all their nuclear facilities and installations under international safeguards—which incurs a responsibility to open these facilities to international inspection. Both the United States and the Soviet Union have been vigorous in urging United Nations Member States to adhere to the terms of the treaty and associated safeguards requirements.

The combination of Nonproliferation Treaty and International Atomic Energy Agency safeguards served as a promising beginning in efforts to inhibit horizontal escalation. However, by the mid-1970s, the advance of technology led to heightened concern in the international community about the adequacy of the safeguards regime that had been established. This concern was heightened by the Indian nuclear explosion in 1974. Subsequently, the U.S. launched discussions with nuclear supplier nations—including the Soviet Union, Japan, and several Western European nations—for the purpose of buttressing existing rules and procedures for the export of nuclear supplies, components, and technology. These discussions led to the formation, in 1977, of the fifteen-nation London Suppliers Group, which endorsed a series of principles intended to govern nuclear technology trade and to strengthen existing safeguards. The norms that emerged have been subject to frequent review and revision. The United States is pledged to support these endeavors and, wherever possible, to develop additional rules and restraints for the export of sensitive nuclear technologies, material, and equipment.

Consonant with pledges of the United States, the Congress formulated the Nuclear Nonproliferation Act, which was signed into law by President Carter on March 10, 1978. The act establishes specific criteria for nuclear exports and well-defined, restrictive procedures for the approval of exports of nuclear technology and material. As outlined by the U.S. government in a report on the subject:

> By extending the reach of U.S. law, the act ensures much stricter U.S. controls on nuclear commerce between third countries and states receiving U.S. exports. It also provides a stronger congressional role in U.S. export policy, by requiring congressional approval for some actions and by allowing congressional vetoes over certain executive branch decisions. Under the act, non-nuclear weapons countries seeking U.S. nuclear cooperation or U.S. exports of nuclear facilities, fuel, or technologies, must accept IAEA [International Atomic Energy Agency] safeguards on all of their peaceful nuclear facilities—the so-called full-scale or comprehensive safeguards.[4]

The United States, in compliance with the provisions of the Nuclear Nonproliferation Act of 1978 (section 404), has launched efforts to renegotiate agreements of cooperation with nations seeking exports of U.S. nuclear material and technology. These efforts are clearly intended to enhance a regime of full-scope safeguards under the auspices of the International Atomic Energy Agency. At the same time, the U.S. Department of Energy issued revised and strengthened regulations that serve to control the transfer of unclassified nuclear technology.

The United States, in an effort to demonstrate its strong support for nonproliferation measures in the international community, has undertaken a number of other, ancillary actions. The voluntary offer by the United States, presented to the United Nations in 1978, to accept safeguards on civil nuclear reactors entered into force in 1980. Under this offer, four U.S. facilities were selected by the International Atomic Energy Agency for the application of safeguards, and in 1982, detailed arrangements were negotiated under which these facilities are subject to periodic inspection. Bilateral consultations have also been an important factor in U.S. nonproliferation strategy. During 1982 and 1983, U.S. officials consulted with more than a dozen countries in Europe, Latin America, and Asia on ways to pursue more effectively the common goal of preventing proliferation. During these discussions, particular note was taken of the need to improve nuclear export controls, especially for dual-use commodities—items that have both conventional and potential nuclear uses. These pourparlers have led to a widening appreciation of the dual-use problem and have contributed significantly to an improved nonproliferation approach on the part of the United States. Along the same lines, the United States has addressed with other supplier nations steps that might be taken to impede efforts by sensitive countries—that is, nonadherents of the Nonproliferation Treaty—to acquire the technology and material necessary to pursue a nuclear weapons capability. Agreements have been concluded with several supplier nations to defer or otherwise refuse specific export transactions of proliferation concern. During the 1982 calendar year alone, approximately 100 export alerts among the participating supplier nations were issued and appropriate actions taken; in 1983, the number approached 75 such alerts.

The issue of spent nuclear fuels and wastes has also been addressed and appropriate action taken by the United States. Thus, under section 223 of the Nuclear Waste Policy Act of 1982, a *Federal Register* notice has been published offering to augment U.S. international cooperative arrangements in the area of spent fuel storage and disposal. Nonnuclear weapons states have been approached through diplomatic channels to solicit expressions of interest. To further these objectives, the United States was the host for a major International Atomic Energy Agency international conference on radioactive waste management in Seattle, Washington (May 1983). Of particular significance as well, President Reagan has sought and obtained enactment of domestic U.S. legislation making certain acts involving nuclear material a serious criminal offense. The enacted legislation implements provisions of the international Convention of the Physical Protection of Nuclear Material, which the United States ratified in 1982. The convention represents significant progress in the community of nations in efforts to deal with threats of nuclear terrorism and proliferation. The U.S. government remains fully committed in its efforts to secure the cooperation of other countries to assure adequate physical security where nuclear materials of U.S. origin are involved.

The United States and the Soviet Union have held several bilateral meetings on a broad range of nonproliferation issues. The first of these, under the auspices of the Reagan Administration, was held in Washington in December 1982, and the second was held in Moscow in June 1983. Matters discussed included prospects for strengthening the international nonproliferation regime, assuring the safe development of nuclear energy, and encouraging additional countries to sign the Nonproliferation Treaty and the newly established Convention for the Physical Security of Nuclear Materials. Discussions were also launched on measures that might be proposed to strengthen the capabilities and performance of the International Atomic Energy Agency. The United States and the Soviet Union agreed that the agency safeguards system was crucial to the success of the international nonproliferation regime. They agreed to work in concert on steps to be taken to strengthen that system; both parties also agreed that other agency-sponsored activities should be strongly supported. The Soviet Union expressed support for the concept of comprehensive safeguards, as recommended by President Reagan, but presumed that the policy could not become fully effective until all nuclear suppliers adopt it. On export issues, the discussions produced general agreement. The United States and the Soviet Union share the view that meaningful controls over nuclear exports can make an important contribution to achieving common nonproliferation objectives. Equally noteworthy have been bilateral discussions on comparable matters that have been initiated between the United States and the People's Republic of China. These also promise to produce unanimity of view on critical matters relating to horizontal proliferation and common policies to preclude an expansion in the number of nuclear weapons states.

Plutonium use has been a subject of growing concern to several nations and associations—most notably, EURATOM (European Atomic Energy Community) and Japan. Intensive reviews occurred within the U.S. government with respect to policies under which the United States exercises its consent right over reprocessing of U.S.-origin fuel and plutonium in other countries. As a result of the review, President Reagan authorized discussions to negotiate procedures with Japan and EURATOM for advance long-term consent to retransfers, reprocessing, and use of nuclear material over which the United States has consent rights. The consensus that emerges from these discussions will require new or amended cooperation agreements that are subject to congressional review. The agreements must also be subject to strong commitment by the negotiating nations to nonproliferation efforts and to more effective controls over plutonium.

President Reagan has reaffirmed that adherence and agreement to the Nonproliferation Treaty, the Treaty of Tlatelolco, and supplier agreements for full-scope safeguards, as a condition for significant nuclear cooperation, are essential elements of United States nonproliferation policy. On March 31, 1983, he noted:

> For arms control to be truly complete and world security strengthened . . .
> we must also increase our efforts to halt the spread of nuclear weapons.
> Every country that values a peaceful world must play its part.[5]

There is a general acceptance in the international community that the spread of nuclear weapons must be avoided since it is increasingly evident that proliferation would add to the insecurity of nations, enlarge the divisions that currently exist in various regions, and contribute to vastly greater instability in the international community. A consensus is growing among the 119 signatories and adherents to the Nonproliferation Treaty that the acquisition of nuclear weapons is an imprudent policy course for nations to pursue. Consequently, acknowledgment has grown that the only prudent policy where nuclear programs are involved is a regime of adequate safeguards and ancillary arrangements to make clear each nation's commitment to use the atom for peaceful purposes.

There is comparable recognition among an increasing number of supplier nations that competition must be conducted in a manner that does not impede the effective application of safeguards. However, the prospective emergence of new suppliers adds even greater urgency to the efforts of the United Nations, the United States, the Soviet Union, and others to preserve and strengthen the agreed rules of nuclear commerce. If disharmony were to materialize among existing suppliers on conditions for nuclear export, new suppliers may be tempted to use nonproliferation conditions as a bargaining factor in their pursuit of market opportunities. Successful safeguards and cooperation among existing supplier nations will diminish this risk, and they hope, impel new supplier nations to adhere to strengthened safeguards and procedures currently under contemplation.

Under existing circumstances, the United Nations, nuclear weapons nations, nuclear technology and materials supplier nations, and regional official organizations can work together to reinforce measures and steps needed to diminish the chances of proliferation. Among the measures to be considered are the following:

Reinforcement of efforts to secure adherence to the Nonproliferation Treaty and the Treaty of Tlatelolco by all interested parties;

Strengthening of the safeguard provisions and responsibilities of the International Atomic Energy Agency;

Expansion in the number of civilian nuclear facilities that are subject to on-site inspection by agency officials, as well as placement of monitors at facilities where the possibility of weapons research appears likely;

Negotiation of an international agreement by all of the nuclear weapons states to foreswear use of military weapons of mass destruction in the event of hostilities or conflicts with nonnuclear weapons states.

Ultimately, however, safeguards and efforts to diminish the likelihood of proliferation involve more than a simple signature on treaties, codicils, or other official documents. To demonstrate its bona fides, each nation must also make both a formal commitment to peace and undertake actions that produce confidence in such commitments. Denial of nuclear technology can only delay the spread of nuclear weapons of war; only political accommodation and mutual confidence in the peaceful policies of the United Nations Member States can permanently prevent the spread of these catastrophic weapons to the inventories of the nations that are unable to resolve local or regional security concerns through peaceful means. The U.S. government is pledged to find appropriate measure, in collaboration with like-minded nations, to diminish these security concerns and thereby to engender confidence in security through peace and respect for the norms that insure international order.

NOTES

1. See United Nations, *Comprehensive Study on Nuclear Weapons*, No. E.81 (New York: United Nations, 1965).
2. U.S. Department of State Bulletin No. 3 (Washington, D.C.: GPO, July 1981).
3. Address by the Honorable Richard T. Kennedy before the Atomic Industrial Forum and FORATOM, Geneva, Switzerland, June 1, 1983 (Washington, D.C.: U.S. State Department Bulletin No. 5.)
4. U.S. Department of State, *Security and Arms Control* (Washington, D.C.: GPO, 1983), p. 61.
5. U.S. Department of State Bulletin No. 6 (Washington, D.C.: GPO, April 15, 1983), p. 17.

Chapter 5

The Role of Nongovernmental
Organizations

The record of humankind suggests that hostility among peoples, tribes, clans, or nations has been resolved by the adoption of one of several strategies. Parties that feel threatened may capitulate to a stronger adversary. This strategy has certain limitations since capitulation has often spelled annihilation or extinction of the corporate identity of the group wishing to embrace a doctrine of unconditional surrender. Other strategies have proved more attractive. One involves the acquisition of military means to counter or effectively neutralize the capabilities of a perceived adversary. Security through acquired military might necessitates the allocation of human resources and treasures to the military sector and, in some instances, alliance formation. A second, or alternate, strategy is less costly but entails significant risk taking. This strategy involves dependence on arms limitation, the general disposition being to search for a basis for restraint in the cause of peace. The first strategy offers a measure of security but leaves open the possibility of ongoing competition for power—with the undesirable possibility being recourse by one of the adversaries to force of arms to resolve disputes. The alternative strategy offers the prospect of long-term security but requires assurances that none of the parties to a dispute intends to use or is capable of using military force to impose its solution to an ongoing disagreement.

Based on previous experience, some national leaders regard an arms limitation strategy as either utopian, in the sense of being impossible of attainment in the turbulent contemporary international environment, or so remote in terms of ultimate achievement that they are unwilling to accept the risks associated with such a strategy. They would insist on a litmus test involving the prior resolution of outstanding political issues together with confidence-building measures as preconditions for acceptance of this strategy.

Most statesmen would observe, however, that disarmament and security are neither incompatible nor mutually unattainable objectives. As Professor Richard Smoke of the United States has observed:

> [A]n unarmed or largely unarmed world would be a far more secure place than the quite dangerous one in which we actually live. Since many Americans think of this as a visionary ideal—a dream of a distant, Utopian future—rather than an image of national security, it bears repeating: *The national security of the United States* would be incomparably greater in a world in which *no nation,* including the United States, possessed significant military power. (Here "significant" simply means that any country will always want to retain enough police and national guard forces to deal with crime and internal disturbances.) Quite apart from other advantages in living in such a world, the American people would be more secure than any time in the recent past—including times when the United States enjoyed strategic superiority—or than they would be in any future world of armed powers and superpowers.[1]

Because of the absence of an environment of peace and cooperation between the superpowers, the United States has relied on a combination of military strength to protect its vital interests—as well as those of friends and allies, within the framework of collective security—and support for policies and strategies calling for arms control. From time to time, the U.S. government also has called for total disarmament in several fields. The most recent of these U.S. initiatives, in 1983, before the United Nations Conference on Disarmament, came in the form of a proposal to ban the development, production, and stockpiling of chemical weapons. Early in 1984, the U.S. delegation prepared a draft treaty calling for the destruction of existing stockpiles of chemical weapons and of production facilities by stages over 10 years, with international inspection arrangements to insure compliance. Of critical importance from the U.S. perspective is an acceptable verification and compliance framework since stockpiles are not susceptible to comprehensive (continuous) monitoring without on-site inspection. Comparable initiatives have been launched in bilateral negotiations between the United States and the Soviet Union with respect to strategic nuclear weapons and theater nuclear weapons, but these have been rejected out of hand by the Soviet Union—both within the confines of the bilateral processes and, in recurring public breaches of diplomatic etiquette, at the United Nations Conference on Disarmament.

Efforts to develop international support for control over nuclear weapons development have been relatively successful. Within the United States and Western Europe, a considerable body of public sentiment has emerged in favor of elimination of all nuclear weapons. Beginning in the United Kingdom, in the 1950s, a small but vociferous ban-the-bomb movement attracted wide attention through public meetings and demonstrations, using the slogan "Better red than dead." Sentiment of a more moderate persuasion expressed its support for a process that would not be so one dimensional—that is, unilateral disarmament on the part of the United States and those NATO member states that regarded the U.S. nuclear umbrella as an effective deterrent against aggression by the Warsaw Treaty Organization. With the growth of national security studies on U.S. and Western European campuses, together with the burgeoning of advanced research centers, other, more prudent proposals in the disarmament field began to emerge. One involved the so-called strategy of minimum deterrence. Under this strategy the United States would divest itself unilaterally of the preponderance of its strategic nuclear arsenal but retain approximately 200 secure missiles to provide credibility to U.S. security commitments to allies against attack by the Warsaw Treaty Organization. Thereafter, the United States would proceed to negotiate total elimination of nuclear arsenals with the Soviet Union. The underlying assumption of advocates of disarmament was that a stable relationship could not be established and maintained between the superpowers as long as both disposed of massive nuclear weapons arsenals. The pressure of international events, together with the imperatives of scientific research and technological breakthroughs, would always serve to threaten whatever equilibrium might be established. In brief, almost ineluctably, arms competition would produce ongoing nuclear competition. Inherent in this approach was the belief that even if small nuclear arsenals could be vouchsafed and the doctrine of deterrence were to fail, the damage visited on international society by a limited nuclear exchange would not spell the annihilation of international society in its existing form.

The other general view of the deterrent relationship was that it could . . . remain stable, if not forever, at least for a long time during which much might change. This was the opinion of the majority of analysts in the late 1950s and has remained the mainstream view within the field since. The majority of national security specialists in America have always been more concerned with the adequacy of American efforts to deter Soviet attacks than with the long-term feasibility of deterrence per se.[2]

As the 1960s began, the prevalent U.S. view was that a delicate balance of terror had been established between the United States and the Soviet Union, assuring secure second strike capabilities; hence, the competition that had fueled the arms race should abate. Forces of moderation and restraint would now override future competition and generate movement toward agreement on arms control and disarmament. These extravagant expectations were fueled as the decade came to a close—hallmarked by general superpower strategic parity—by the onset of a period of détente and the beginning of SALT. A wide variety of nongovernmental organizations in the United States and Western Europe were encouraged by these developments.

A subtle shift did occur as the process of arms control talks reached full flower in the 1970s. The two superpowers, rather than concentrate their efforts on total disarmament, focused their negotiations on ways to slow and eventually halt strategic weapons competition. The prevalent hope was that the negotiating process would produce greater confidence in each party's avowed desire not to utilize nuclear weapons as a means of achieving political leverage. Such confidence would alter in consequence plans for the acquisition of new generations of weapons. In the United States, the hope grew that progressive arms control might serve as a more realistic and effective strategy than efforts to fashion a grand design for immediate and total disarmament. Consonant with this view, national security specialists in U.S nongovernmental organizations began to urge both the U.S. Congress and the Executive Branch to consider defense requirements (including budgetary allocations) and arms control simultaneously when security issues arose. Specialists also began to examine the advisability of selecting new weapons systems for research in the context of delicate arms control negotiations in progress, force structure decisions as a signal to Soviet negotiators of U.S. intentions, and the impact of budget reductions for the U.S. Department of Defense as a means of providing additional impetus to successful completion of negotiations. Unfortunately, these recommendations, when adopted by the United States, found no reciprocity in the Soviet Union. The arsenal of Soviet military weaponry that continued to grow prodigiously in the 1970s, overtures to establish a regime of restraint in the transfer of conventional military equipment to several Third World regions that were frustrated by massive deliveries of Soviet equipment to Third World nations, the use of Soviet troops in Czechoslovakia in 1968, and the invasion of Afghanistan in 1979 served to undermine the confidence in the arms control process as a means of moderating differences and fostering a regime of restraint in superpower relations.

The worsening of the climate of superpower relations over the past several years has led to increased public discussion of the threat to international order and security which is its natural by-product. Growing public concern regarding nuclear war, nuclear weapons programs, and the nuclear arms race has played a significant role in shaping governmental policies in Western Europe. Concern in Europe manifests itself in the peace movement. In the United States, the nuclear freeze campaign and educational activities of groups such as Ground Zero, the Council for a Livable World, the Union of Concerned Scientists, and others have been a catalyst for public discussion and involvement in demonstrations. The statement of U.S. Catholic bishops concerning the moral foundations of nuclear war has also received wide attention in the United States. It is also pertinent that, for the first time since public alarm was expressed over the possibility of strontium-90 in mothers' milk and the capacities of children to function neurologically in the 1960s, large numbers of American women and women's organizations have become involved in nuclear questions. Recent study decisions by the League of Women Voters and the American Association of University Women reflect concern over the growing nuclear arsenals of the United States and the Soviet Union.

In recent years, so-called national security professional organizations also have become involved in the widening debate in the United States and in Western Europe. In the United Kingdom, the late Lord Mountbatten was only the most notable, because in the United Kingdom the list of advocates of arms reductions is impressive. In the United States, the list includes Professor George Kennan, McGeorge Bundy, Robert McNamara, and Gerard Smith.

One must acknowledge that nongovernmental organizations are significant instruments in mobilizing international opinion on arms control issues. Public perceptions of the dangers inherent in the nuclear weapons competition of the superpowers have grown demonstrably in the 1980s. An atmosphere of alarm exists in some nations, with mass movements having been organized over the current parlous situation. Their protests and expressions of concern are well understood, particularly in the United States where a certain resonance has crystallized. These organizations and special interest groups all subscribe to United Nations efforts to prevent nuclear conflict, as expressed in a series of public resolutions and agreements–notably, the Declaration on International Cooperation for Disarmament, the Declaration on the Strengthening of International Security, and the Declaration of the 1980s as the Second Disarmament Decade. Noteworthy, in addition, has been the General Assembly Declaration on the Prevention of Nuclear Catastrophe, adopted at its thirty-sixth session. Many nongovernmental organizations have supported a major moral prescription contained in the latter document: its injunction against all military strategies calling for first use of nuclear weapons in time of tension or armed hostilities.

Once again, however, the question of compliance arises. The military doctrines and strategies of the Soviet Union and the United States do not preclude the use of nuclear weapons (at the tactical level in particular) in war-fighting situations. Such doctrines lower the threshold at which nuclear weapons would be utilized with little assurance that such recourse would not lead to escalation to the strategic level. Nongovernmental organizations in the United States and in Western Europe have called with mounting insistence for a review of such doctrines, the ultimate goals being their elimination from NATO and Warsaw Treaty Organization military planning. The prospect of serious review and eventual revision by 1987 is most promising in the instance of NATO.

Similar action by the Soviet Union and its Warsaw Treaty Organization allies is not likely within the foreseeable future. This lack of congruence of effort underscores a basic dilemma for nongovernmental organizations. While capable of exercising a measure of influence over official organs in Western Europe and the United States, their capacity to develop relationships with groups in the Soviet Union and other Warsaw Treaty Organization nations is negligible. Protest demonstrations against Soviet military doctrine in the Soviet Union and Eastern Europe are proscribed by official organs of government. To date, the efforts of Western peace groups to travel to Warsaw Treaty Organization nations for the purpose of coordinating efforts at public discussion and demonstration have been frustrated. Official objection has aroused suspicion in some quarters that the approach of the Soviet Union to peace and nuclear disarmament movements is one dimensional—that is, the Soviet Union wishes to encourage criticism of governmental policies in the Western democracies while foreclosing on public expressions of dissent on military policies in the Soviet Union and Eastern Europe.

The processes of information dissemination and open discussion, which have been unfettered in the United States and Western Europe, have not been replicated in Warsaw Treaty Organization nations. Communist government actions have been at variance with protestations of support for peace movements that operate without inhibition in noncommunist nations. A few examples are noteworthy:

1. In Czechoslovakia, members of the Charter of 77, a group that is anxious to support the Helsinki accords and the Charter of the United Nations, have been subject to harassment and arrest since the organization was formed.
2. In the German Democratic Republic, peace movements that use sym-

bolic arm patches showing the beating of swords into ploughshares are periodically denounced by German authorities. Workers and students publicly displaying such symbols are expelled from schools and denied opportunities to secure employment.

3. Efforts on the part of peace supporters to disseminate the views of Andrei Sakharov, a Soviet citizen and Nobel Peace Prize laureate, have been interdicted by Soviet authorities, and Mr. Sakharov has been subjected to enforced residence away from his family as a result of his independence of view.

In August 1982, a Pugwash Conference, which had its venue in Warsaw, Poland, circulated a letter by Mr. Sakharov. The subject of his open letter was the widening arms race and the need for open discussion of the responsibilities of the United States and the Soviet Union in reducing world tensions. In regard to the arms race, the Sakharov letter read:

> In the last decade there has been a very substantial increase in the Soviet army, navy, missile arsenal and air force, while the countries of the West, Europe especially, have weakened their defense efforts. The SS-20 missiles have changed the strategic equilibrium in Europe, although those who take part in pacifist demonstrations seem not to notice this fact.[3]

Mr. Sakharov concluded his letter to the Pugwash Conference—a letter which the Polish government refused to accept for publication—that: "There must be international efforts, efforts made by all honest people, to defend human rights, to overcome the closed nature of the USSR and other socialist countries."[4] This plea merits very serious consideration by United Nations Member States if the cause of peace and disarmament is to progress and to achieve positive results.

The record of peaceful cooperation is even more distressing when efforts to forge transnational ties by nongovernmental organizations are considered. In mid-1982, the largest peaceful disarmament rallies in the history of the United States occurred in New York City and communities throughout the United States. In the wake of these rallies, eleven Soviet citizens announced plans to organize a unique, independent disarmament group to be called the Group to Establish Trust between the U.S.A. and the U.S.S.R. Very much in the spirit of the recommendations of the working group at the second special session on disarmament, the proposal to form such a collaborative venture met with an enthusiastic response in the United States. However, the Soviet Union reacted negatively, arresting several members of the group of eleven for hooliganism. One member was confined for thirty days in a psychiatric institute where he reportedly was treated with debilitating drugs. In September 1983, the same date that the government of the Soviet Union announced that it would boycott future meetings on intermediate-range nuclear weapons in Geneva, the Soviet Union announced the trial of the leader of the trust group, Mr. Oleg Radzinsky, who had previously been arrested for anti-Soviet agitation. On December 8, 1983, the day the Soviet Union announced that it would no longer participate in the START negotiations dealing with strategic nuclear weapons systems, the Soviet Union also announced that it had brought charges against a cofounder of the Trust Group, Olga Medvedkova, while threatening to take legal action against six other members.[5]

What is of more than passing interest is that, despite official harassment, the urge for peace and disarmament in the Soviet Union has led to a significant growth in the membership of the Trust Group. From an original circle of eleven, the movement now claims 2,000 active supporters in nine major cities in the Soviet Union. The record is clear regarding the lack of interest by the government of the Soviet Union in the creation of nongovernmental bonds by individuals and groups dedicated to the cause of peace. Transnational cooperation represents a threat to state security when it falls outside the boundaries of state control. Moreover, it can produce dissidence of a destabilizing nature to certain types of political systems. Apparently, the constant call for confidence building has no resonance where nongovernmental organizations are likely to develop independence of judgment; the danger is of new "refusnik" groups and demonstrations developing outside official control. Dissent, public criticism, and demonstrations are a phenomenon to be welcomed and greeted with benevolence only in democratic societies.

The situation of harassment of independent-minded Soviet citizens achieved such a point of unacceptability that arms control and disarmament groups in the United States and in Western Europe have felt compelled to register their distress. Thus, on September 20, 1982, American leaders of the movement to freeze Soviet and U.S. nuclear arsenals—including the chairman for the Council for a Livable World and an American member of the Soviet Union's Academy of Sciences—dispatched a letter to former President Leonid I. Brezhnev protesting Soviet actions against their Soviet colleagues in the peace movement. The leaders of the U.S. freeze movement received no response assuring that the government of the Soviet Union would recede from its efforts to intimidate groups wishing to establish independent ties with their U.S. counterparts.[6]

Efforts to achieve a community of spirit and a general consensus on arms control and disarmament through the vehicle of nongovernmental organizations are at a critical juncture. Despite the agreements that have been concluded under the auspices of the United Nations, by regional groups such as the Latin American states and bilaterally by the United

States and the Soviet Union, the arsenals of the superpowers and of France, the United Kingdom, and the Republic of China have grown even more lethal since the 1960s. As a result, U.S. and Soviet citizens, the populations of Eastern and Western Europe, and those not enmeshed directly in East-West disagreements are less secure today than they have been since the founding of the United Nations. The total destructive power that the Soviet Union can visit upon the United States, already sufficient to destroy all major U.S. cities as the 1970s began, is currently so huge that it threatens the United States and every one of its friends and allies with complete annihilation. Similarly, the United States disposes of sufficient nuclear weaponry to insure the obliteration of Soviet civilization. Indeed, a full-scale nuclear exchange between the two superpowers would effectively threaten all human beings on earth.

What, then, is the constructive role that nongovernmental organizations can play in diminishing the chances of nuclear war? Initially, they must search for means to secure international recognition and acceptance as representatives of concerned citizenry. Such acceptance exists in the United States and in Western Europe, as well as in a variety of nations in Latin America, Africa, and Asia. It requires extension into Eastern Europe and the Soviet Union as well.

Second, a litmus test of acceptance in the Soviet Union must be a change in the official posture of the government of the Soviet Union with respect to the right of its citizens to organize and to debate arms control and disarmament issues outside the shadow of bureaucratic control. Absent such right, the protestations of Soviet support for disarmament lacks credibility in the United Nations and in the West generally.

Third, nongovernmental organizations must be permitted unfettered access to one another for the express purpose of exchanging information and establishing agreed agendas for common action. These agendas, to be realistic, must address the official policies and programs of nuclear weapons states with a view to urging changes in posture or position where the latter are deemed requisite for the cause of international peace.

Fourth, dissent or opposition to governmental policies must be permitted. To do otherwise is to constrict the actions of nongovernmental organizations and, in the majority of cases, to transform such organizations into instruments of propaganda. The end result is to produce a double standard, one which erodes the willingness of governments in the West to accede to the recommendations of nongovernmental organizations in their own societies. These basic measures, if accepted and acted upon, will provide fresh inspiration and renewed momentum to the international movement for peace and disarmament.

Inevitably, then, a nexus exists between the official policies and actions of nations publicly committed to the prevention of nuclear war, and the opportunity to organize, debate, and criticize official policies by nongovernmental organizations. Regional organizations and international movements can play a constructive role in securing free and unfettered discussion of disarmament issues by nongovernmental organizations. The Nonaligned Movement has taken cognizance of its potential in this area. In 1983, at the seventh summit conference, convened in India, Prime Minister Indira Gandhi proposed that the movement consider new initiatives that might be sponsored to increase public awareness of international tensions that have arisen and the dangers that attend these tensions. Quite conceivably, the Nonaligned Movement would be prepared to help organize conferences on a regional basis, involving local citizenry, to address the dangers and to fashion an action program, involving nongovernmental organizations, to mobilize sentiment in favor of arms control and disarmament. An integral part of this action program should be the unhindered flow of information to all peoples of the world and assurance of the widest possible freedom of public expression and assembly on the crucial issues that confront the inhabitants of the planet earth.

NOTES

1. Richard Smoke, *National Security and the Nuclear Dilemma* (New York: Addison-Wesley, 1984), p. 128.
2. Ibid., p. 135.
3. Reported in U.S. Department of State, "Current Policy," Publication no. 440 (Washington, D.C.: GPO, 1982). pp. 7–8.
4. Ibid. pp. 7–8.
5. Speech by Ambassador Kenneth Adelman, First Committee, U.N. General Assembly, November 4, 1982 (Washington, D.C.: U.S. Department of State), pp. 2–3.
6. Ibid., pp. 2–3.

Chapter 6

Conclusion

The apocalyptic revelation associated with the dawning of the nuclear age should have inspired statesmen of prudence and moderation to redouble their efforts to surrender a measure of their sovereignty to the United Nations and thereby to find safety from the new weapons of mass destruction. For a variety of reasons, the risks of delegated authority proved greater than the temptations of security through autonomous arms development programs. The logic of short-sighted statesmanship has been fulfilled. Today, there are more than 50,000 nuclear warheads in the inventories of five nations, and the number both of warheads and of new nuclear weapons states may grow over the 1990s. Existing inventories possess a destructive power 1.7 million times greater than the atomic weapon that wrought riveting devastation at Nagasaki and Hiroshima.

The world is spiritually impoverished by the dawn of the nuclear age. Humankind lives in the shadow of an increasing vulnerability, one in which fear inspired by the threat of nuclear cataclysm is ever present. Today, there is widening debate about whether the nuclear arms race is a special cause or a major symptom of the tensions that have arisen among the nuclear weapons states. Close examination of the subject should lead to the inescapable conclusion that the accumulation of nuclear arms is not a cause of international tensions but is one of its direct consequences. It follows, therefore, that disarmament negotiations, if they are to be successful, must be preceded or accompanied by progress in the resolution of global and superpower issues.

President Reagan, in a foreign policy address at the White House (Washington, D.C.), on January 16, 1984, took cognizance of the underlying problem. Characterizing 1984 as a year of opportunities for peace, he urged the Soviet Union to join the United States to rise to the challenges facing them by finding areas of mutual interest and building on them. He proposed that the two governments:

1. Find ways to reduce and eventually to eliminate the threat and use of force in solving international disputes.
2. Find ways to reduce the vast stockpiles of armaments in the world. This would include existing stockpiles of nuclear weapons.
3. Enter into a commitment for continuing dialogue between the United States and the Soviet Union as a way to strengthen foundations for peaceful coexistence.

In the classic definition of international politics, nations sought through the balance of power to achieve two objectives: (1) the preservation of their own existence and (2), when possible, the maintenance of peace in the international system. In the past, these two goals have appeared incompatible. As the twentieth century enters its concluding years, the two goals are indistinguishable. Nuclear war is a worse contingency than any injustices or transgressions it seeks to correct. The peoples of the small planet earth may have a greater appreciation of the dangers inherent in mounting disagreements and tensions. The most urgent requirement of our day is the recognition of the dangers by statesmen and diplomats and the need to search with yet greater diligence for the measures to be embraced for the salvation of humankind. The opportunities and challenges are clearly before us; the hope and expectation must be that national leaders will have the foresight and wisdom to act in accordance with the wishes of the overwhelming majority of their citizens.

Appendix A

ADDRESS BY PRESIDENT REAGAN BEFORE THE THIRTY-NINTH SESSION OF THE GENERAL ASSEMBLY, SEPTEMBER 24, 1984

Mr. President, Mr. Secretary-General, distinguished heads of state, ministers, representatives, and guests:

First of all, I wish to congratulate President Lusaka on his election as President of the General Assembly. I wish you every success, Mr. President, in carrying out the responsibilities of this high international office.

It's an honor to be here, and I thank you for your gracious invitation. I would speak in support of the two great goals that led to the formation of this organization—the cause of peace and the cause of human dignity.

The responsibility of this Assembly—the peaceful resolution of disputes between peoples and nations—can be discharged successfully only if we recognize the great common ground upon which we all stand: our fellowship as members of the human race, our oneness as inhabitants of this planet, our place as representatives of billions of our countrymen whose fondest hope remains the end to war and to the repression of the human spirit. These are the important central realities that bind us, that permit us to dream of a future without the antagonisms of the past. And just as shadows can be seen only where there is light, so, too, can we overcome what is wrong only if we remember how much is right. And we will resolve what divides us only if we remember how much more unites us.

This chamber has heard enough about the problems and dangers ahead. Today, let us dare to speak of a future that is bright and hopeful and can be ours only if we seek it. I believe that future is far nearer than most of us would dare to hope.

At the start of this decade, one scholar at the Hudson Institute noted that mankind also had undergone enormous changes for the better in the past two centuries—changes which aren't always readily noticed or written about.

"Up until 200 years ago, there were relatively few people in the world," he wrote. "All human societies were poor. Disease and early death dominated most people's lives. People were ignorant, and largely at the mercy of the forces of nature."

"Now," he said, "we are somewhere near the middle of a process of economic development.... At the end of that process almost no one will live in a country as poor as the richest country of the past. There will be many more people . . . living long, healthy lives, with immense knowledge and more to learn than any-body has time for." They will be "able to cope with the forces of nature and almost indifferent to distance."

Well, we do live today, as the scholar suggested, in the middle of one of the most important and dramatic periods in human history—one in which all of us can serve as catalysts for an era of world peace and unimagined human freedom and dignity.

And today I would like to report to you, as distinguished and influential mem-bers of the world community, on what the United States has been attempting to do to help move the world closer to this era. On many fronts enormous prog-ress has been made, and I think our efforts are complemented by the trend of history.

If we look closely enough, I believe we can see all the world moving toward a deeper appreciation of the value of human freedom in both its political and economic manifestations. This is partially motivated by a worldwide desire for economic growth and higher standards of living. And there's an increasing reali-zation that economic freedom is a prelude to economic progress and growth and is intricately and inseparably linked to political freedom.

Everywhere, people and governments are beginning to recognize that the secret of a progressive new world is to take advantage of the creativity of the human spirit, to encourage innovation and individual enterprise, to reward hard work, and to reduce barriers to the free flow of trade and information.

Our opposition to economic restrictions and trade barriers is consistent with our view of economic freedom and human progress. We believe such barriers pose a particularly dangerous threat to the developing nations and their chance to share in world prosperity through expanded export markets. Tomorrow at the International Monetary Fund, I will address this question more fully, including America's desire for more open trading markets throughout the world.

This desire to cut down trade barriers and our open advocacy of freedom as the engine of human progress are two of the most important ways the United States and the American people hope to assist in bringing about a world where prosperity is commonplace, conflict an aberration, and human dignity and free-dom a way of life.

Let me place these steps more in context by briefly outlining the major goals of American foreign policy and then exploring with you the practical ways we're attempting to further freedom and prevent war: By that I mean, first, how we have moved to strengthen ties with old allies and new friends; second, what we're doing to help avoid the regional conflicts that could contain the seeds of world conflagration; and third, the status of our efforts with the Soviet Union to reduce the level of arms.

Let me begin with a word about the objectives of American foreign policy, which have been consistent since the postwar era, and which fueled the formation of the United Nations and were incorporated into the U.N. Charter itself.

The U.N. Charter states two overriding goals: "to save succeeding generations from the scourge of war, which twice in our lifetime has brought untold sorrow to mankind," and "to reaffirm faith in fundamental human rights, in the dignity and worth of the human person, in the equal rights of men and women and of nations large and small."

The founders of the United Nations understood full well the relationship between these two goals. And I want you to know that the Government of the United States will continue to view this concern for human rights as the moral center of our foreign policy. We can never look at anyone's freedom as a bargaining chip in world politics. Our hope is for a time when all the people of the world can enjoy the blessings of personal liberty. But I would like also to emphasize that our concern for protecting human rights is part of our concern for protecting the peace.

The answer is for all nations to fulfill the obligations they freely assumed under the Universal Declaration of Human Rights. It states, "The will of the people shall be the basis of the authority of government; this will shall be expressed in periodic and genuine elections." The Declaration also includes these rights: "to form and to join trade unions," "to own property alone as well as in association with others," "to leave any country including his own and return to his country," and to enjoy "freedom of opinion and expression." Perhaps the most graphic example of the relationship between human rights and peace is the right of peace groups to exist and to promote their views. In fact, the treatment of peace groups may be a litmus test of government's true desire for peace.

In addition to emphasizing this tie between the advocacy of human rights and the prevention of war, the United States has taken important steps, as I mentioned earlier, to prevent world conflict. The starting point and cornerstone of our foreign policy is our alliance and partnership with our fellow democracies. For 35 years, the North Atlantic alliance has guaranteed the peace in Europe. In both Europe and Asia, our alliances have been the vehicle for a great reconciliation among nations that had fought bitter wars in decades and centuries past. And here in the Western Hemisphere, North and South are being lifted on the tide of freedom and are joined in a common effort to foster peaceful economic development.

We're proud of our association with all those countries that share our commitment to freedom, human rights, the rule of law, and international peace. Indeed, the bulwark of security that the democratic alliance provides is essential and remains essential to the maintenance of world peace. Every alliance involves burdens and obligations, but these are far less than the risks and sacrifices that will result if the peace-loving nations were divided and neglectful of their common security.

The people of the United States will remain faithful to their commitments. But the United States is also faithful to its alliances and friendships with scores of nations in the developed and developing worlds with differing political systems, cultures, and traditions. The development of ties between the United States and China, a significant global event of the last dozen years, shows our willingness to improve relations with countries ideologically very different from ours.

We're ready to be the friend of any country that is a friend to us and a friend of peace. And we respect genuine nonalignment. Our own nation was born in revolution. We helped promote the process of decolonization that brought about the independence of so many members of this body. And we're proud of that history.

We're proud, too, of our role in the formation of the United Nations and our support of this body over the years. And let me again emphasize our unwavering commitment to a central principle of the United Nations system—the principle of universality, both here and in the United Nations technical agencies around the world. If universality is ignored, if nations are expelled illegally, then the U.N. itself cannot be expected to succeed.

The United States welcomes diversity and peaceful competition. We do not fear the trends of history. We are not ideologically rigid. We do have principles, and we will stand by them, but we will also seek the friendship and good will of all, both old friends and new.

We've always sought to lend a hand to help others—from our relief efforts in Europe after World War I to the Marshall Plan and massive foreign assistance programs after World War II. Since 1946 the United States has provided over $115 billion in economic aid to developing countries, and today provides about one-third of the nearly $90 billion in financial resources, public and private, that flows to the developing world. And the U.S. imports about one-third of the manufactured exports of the developing world.

But any economic progress as well as any movement in the direction of greater understanding between the nations of the world are, of course, endangered by the prospect of conflict at both the global and regional level. In a few minutes, I will turn to the menace of conflict on a worldwide scale and discuss the status of negotiations between the United States and the Soviet Union. But permit me first to address the critical problem of regional conflicts; for history displays tragic evidence that it is these conflicts which can set off the sparks leading to worldwide conflagration.

In a glass display case across the hall from the Oval Office at the White House there is a gold medal, the Nobel Peace Prize won by Theodore Roosevelt for his contribution in mediating the Russo-Japanese War in 1905. It was the first such prize won by an American, and it's part of a tradition of which the American people are very proud—a tradition that is being continued today in many regions of the globe.

We're engaged, for example, in diplomacy to resolve conflicts in southern Africa, working with the Front Line States and our partners in the Contact Group. Mozambique and South Africa have reached an historic accord on nonaggression and cooperation. South Africa and Angola have agreed on a disengagement of forces from Angola, and the groundwork has been laid for the independence of Namibia, with virtually all aspects of Security Council Resolution 435 agreed upon.

Let me add that the United States considers it a moral imperative that South Africa's racial policies evolve peacefully but decisively toward a system compatible with basic norms of justice, liberty, and human dignity. I'm pleased that American companies in South Africa, by providing equal employment opportunities, are contributing to the economic advancement of the black population. But, clearly, much more must be done.

In Central America, the United States has lent support to a diplomatic process to restore regional peace and security. We have committed substantial resources to promote economic development and social progress.

The growing success of democracy in El Salvador is the best proof that the key to peace lies in a political solution. Free elections brought into office a government dedicated to democracy, reform, economic progress, and regional peace. Regrettably, there are forces in the region eager to thwart democratic change, but these forces are now on the defensive. The tide is turning in the direction of freedom. We call upon Nicaragua, in particular, to abandon its policies of subversion and militarism and to carry out the promises it made to the Organization of American States to establish democracy at home.

The Middle East has known more than its share of tragedy and conflict for decades, and the United States has been actively involved in peace diplomacy for just as long. We consider ourselves a full partner in the quest for peace. The record of the 11 years since the October War shows that much can be achieved through negotiations; it also shows that the road is long and hard:

–Two years ago, I proposed a fresh start toward a negotiated solution to the Arab-Israeli conflict. My initiative of September 1, 1982, contains a set of positions that can serve as a basis for a just and lasting peace. That initiative remains a realistic and workable approach, and I am committed to it as firmly as on the day I announced it. And the foundation stone of this effort remains Security Council Resolution 242, which in turn was incorporated in all its parts in the Camp David accords.

–The tragedy of Lebanon has not ended. Only last week, a despicable act of barbarism by some who are unfit to associate with humankind reminded us once again that Lebanon continues to suffer. In 1983 we helped Israel and Lebanon reach an agreement that, if implemented, could have led to the full withdrawal of Israeli forces in the context of the withdrawal of all foreign forces. This agreement was blocked, and the long agony of the Lebanese continues. Thousands of people are still kept from their homes by continued violence and are refugees in their own country. The once flourishing economy of Lebanon is near collapse. All of Lebanon's friends should work together to help end this nightmare.

–In the Gulf, the United States has supported a series of Security Council resolutions that call for an end to the war between Iran and Iraq that has meant so much death and destruction and put the world's economic well-being at risk. Our hope is that hostilities will soon end, leaving each side with its political and territorial integrity intact, so that both may devote their energies to addressing the needs of their people and a return to relationships with other states.

–The lesson of experience is that negotiations work. The peace treaty between Israel and Egypt brought about the peaceful return of the Sinai, clearly showing that the negotiating process brings results when the parties commit themselves to it. The time is bound to come when the same wisdom and courage will be applied with success to reach peace between Israel and all of its Arab neighbors in a manner that assures security for all in the region, the recognition of Israel, and a solution to the Palestinian problem.

In every part of the world, the United States is similarly engaged in peace diplomacy as an active player or a strong supporter:

–In Southeast Asia, we have backed the efforts of ASEAN to mobilize international support for a peaceful resolution of the Cambodian problem, which must include the withdrawal of Vietnamese forces and the election of a representative government. ASEAN's success in promoting economic and political development has made a major contribution to the peace and stability of the region.

–In Afghanistan, the dedicated efforts of the Secretary-General and his representatives to find a diplomatic settlement have our strong support. I assure you that the United States will continue to do everything possible to find a negotiated outcome which provides the Afghan people with the right to determine their own destiny, allows the Afghan refugees to return to their own country in dignity, and protects the legitimate security interests of all neighboring countries.

–On the divided and tense Korean peninsula, we have strongly backed the confidence-building measures proposed by the Republic of Korea and by the U.N. Command at Panmunjom. These are an important first step toward peaceful reunification in the long term.

–We take heart from progress by others in lessening the tensions, notably the efforts by the Federal Republic to reduce barriers between the two German states.

–And the United States strongly supports the Secretary-General's efforts to assist the Cypriot parties in achieving a peaceful and reunited Cyprus.

The United States has been and will always be a friend of peaceful solutions. This is no less true with respect to my country's relations with the Soviet Union.

When I appeared before you last year, I noted that we cannot count on the instinct for survival alone to protect us against war. Deterrence is necessary but not sufficient. America has repaired its strength. We have invigorated our alliances and friendships. We are ready for constructive negotiations with the Soviet Union.

We recognize that there is no sane alternative to negotiations on arms control and other issues between our two nations which have the capacity to destroy civilization as we know it. I believe this is a view shared by virtually every country in the world and by the Soviet Union itself. And I want to speak to you today on what the United States and the Soviet Union can accomplish together in the coming years and the concrete steps that we need to take.

You know, as I stand here and look out from this podium, there in front of me I can see the seat of the Representative from the Soviet Union. And not far from that seat, just over to the side, is the seat of the Representative from the United States. In this historic assembly hall, it's clear there's not a great distance between us. Outside this room, while there will still be clear differences, there's every reason why we should do all that is possible to shorten that distance. And that's why we're here. Isn't that what this organization is all about? [Applause]

Last January 16, I set out three objectives for U.S.-Soviet relations that can provide an agenda for our work over the months ahead.

First, I said, we need to find ways to reduce–and eventually to eliminate–the threat and use of force in solving international disputes. Our concern over the potential for nuclear war cannot deflect us from the terrible human tragedies occurring every day in the regional conflicts I just discussed. Together, we have a particular responsibility to contribute to political solutions to these problems, rather than to exacerbate them through the provision of even more weapons.

I propose that our two countries agree to embark on periodic consultations at policy level about regional problems. We will be prepared, if the Soviets agree, to make senior experts available at regular intervals for in depth exchanges of views. I've asked Secretary Shultz to explore this with Foreign Minister Gromyko. Spheres of influence are a thing of the past; differences between American and Soviet interests are not. The objectives of this political dialog will be to help avoid miscalculation, reduce the potential risk of U.S.-Soviet confrontation, and help the people in areas of conflict to find peaceful solutions.

The United States and the Soviet Union have achieved agreements of the historic importance on some regional issues. The Austrian State Treaty and the Berlin accords are notable and lasting examples. Let us resolve to achieve similar agreements in the future.

Our second task must be to find ways to reduce the vast stockpiles of armaments in the world. I am committed to redoubling our negotiating efforts to achieve real results: in Geneva, a complete ban on chemical weapons; in Vienna, real reductions to lower and equal levels in Soviet and American, Warsaw Pact and NATO conventional forces; in Stockholm, concrete practical measures to enhance mutual confidence, to reduce the risk of war, and to reaffirm commitments concerning nonuse of force; in the field of nuclear testing, improvements in verification essential to ensure compliance with the Threshold Test Ban and Peaceful Nuclear Explosions agreements; and in the field of nonproliferation, close cooperation to strengthen the international institutions and practices aimed at halting the spread of nuclear weapons, together with redoubled efforts to meet the legitimate expectations of all nations that the Soviet Union and the United States will substantially reduce their own nuclear arsenals.

We and the Soviets have agreed to upgrade our hotline communications facility, and our discussions of nuclear nonproliferation in recent years have been useful to both sides. We think there are other possibilities for improving communications in this area that deserve serious exploration.

I believe the proposal of the Soviet Union for opening U.S.-Soviet talks in Vienna provided an important opportunity to advance these objectives. We've been prepared to discuss a wide range of issues of concern to both sides, such as the relationship between defensive and offensive forces and what has been called the militarization of space. During the talks, we would consider what measures of restraint both sides might take while negotiations proceed. However, any agreement must logically depend upon our ability to get the competition in offensive arms under control and to achieve genuine stability at substantially lower levels of nuclear arms.

Our approach in all these areas will be designed to take into account concerns the Soviet Union has voiced. It will attempt to provide a basis for an historic breakthrough in arms control. I'm disappointed that we were not able to open our meeting in Vienna earlier this month on the date originally proposed by the Soviet Union. I hope we can begin these talks by the end of the year or shortly thereafter.

The third task I set in January was to establish a better working relationship between the Soviet Union and the United States, one marked by greater cooperation and understanding. We've made some modest progress. We have reached agreements to improve our hotline, extend our 10-year economic agreement, enhance consular cooperation, and explore coordination of search and rescue efforts at sea.

We've also offered to increase significantly the amount of U.S. grain for purchase by the Soviets and to provide the Soviets a direct fishing allocation off U.S. coasts. But there's much more we could do together. I feel particularly strongly about breaking down the barriers between the peoples of the United States and the Soviet Union, and between our political, military, and other leaders.

Now, all of these steps that I've mentioned – and especially the arms control negotiations – are extremely important to a step-by-step process toward peace. But let me also say that we need to extend the arms control process to build a bigger umbrella under which it can operate – a road map, if you will, showing where, during the next 20 years or so, these individual efforts can lead. This can greatly assist step-by-step negotiations and enable us to avoid having all our hopes or expectations ride on any single set or series of negotiations. If progress is temporarily halted at one set of talks, this newly established framework for arms control could help us take up the slack at other negotiations.

Today, to the great end of lifting the dread of nuclear war from the peoples of the Earth, I invite the leaders of the world to join in a new beginning. We need a fresh approach to reducing international tensions. History demonstrates beyond controversy that just as the arms competition has its root in political suspicions and anxieties, so it can be channeled in more stabilizing directions and eventually be eliminated if those political suspicions and anxieties are addressed as well.

Toward this end, I will suggest to the Soviet Union that we institutionalize regular ministerial or cabinet-level meetings between our two countries on the whole agenda of issues before us, including the problem of needless obstacles to understanding. To take but one idea for discussion: In such talks, we could consider the exchange of outlines of 5-year military plans for weapons development and our schedules of intended procurement. We would also welcome the exchange of observers at military exercises and locations. And I propose that we find a way for Soviet experts to come to the United States nuclear test site, and for ours to go to theirs, to measure directly the yields of tests of nuclear weapons. We should work toward having such arrangements in place by next spring. I hope that the Soviet Union will cooperate in this undertaking and reciprocate in a manner that will enable the two countries to establish the basis for verification for effective limits on underground nuclear testing.

I believe such talks could work rapidly toward developing a new climate of policy understanding, one that is essential if crises are to be avoided and real arms control is to be negotiated. Of course, summit meetings have a useful role to play. But they need to be carefully prepared, and the benefit here is that meetings at the ministerial level would provide the kind of progress that is the best preparation for higher level talks between ourselves and the Soviet leaders.

How much progress we will make and at what pace, I cannot say. But we have a moral obligation to try and try again.

Some may dismiss such proposals and my own optimism as simplistic American idealism, and they will point to the burdens of the modern world and to history. Well, yes, if we sit down and catalog year by year, generation by generation, the famines, the plagues, the wars, the invasions mankind has endured, the list will grow so long and the assault on humanity so terrific that it seems too much for the human spirit to bear.

But isn't this narrow and shortsighted and not at all how we think of history? Yes, the deeds of infamy or injustice are all recorded, but what shines out from the pages of history is the daring of the dreamers and the deeds of the builders and the doers. These things make up the stories we tell and pass on to our children. They comprise the most enduring and striking fact about human history—that through the heartbreak and tragedy man has always dared to perceive the outline of human progress, the steady growth in not just the material well-being, but the spiritual insight of mankind.

"There have been tyrants and murderers, and for a time they can seem invincible. But in the end, they always fail [fall].[1] Think on it . . . always. All through history, the way of truth and love has always won." That was the belief and the vision of Mahatma Gandhi. He described that, and it remains today a vision that is good and true.

"All is gift," is said to have been the favorite expression of another great spiritualist, a Spanish soldier who gave up the ways of war for that of love and peace. And if we're to make realities of the two great goals of the United Nations Charter—the dreams of peace and human dignity—we must take to heart these words of Ignatius Loyola; we must pause long enough to contemplate the gifts received from Him who made us: the gift of life, the gift of this world, the gift of each other—and the gift of the present.

It is this present, this time that now we must seize. I leave you with a reflection from Mahatma Gandhi, spoken with those in mind who said that the disputes and conflicts of the modern world are too great to overcome. It was spoken shortly after Gandhi's quest for independence had taken him to Britain.

"I am not conscious of a single experience throughout my 3 months' stay in England and Europe," he said, "that made me feel that after all East is East and West is West. On the contrary, I have been convinced more than ever that human nature is much the same, no matter under what clime it flourishes, and that if you approached people with trust and affection, you would have ten-fold trust and thousand-fold affection returned to you."

For the sake of a peaceful world, a world where human dignity and freedom is respected and enshrined, let us approach each other with ten-fold trust and thousand-fold affection. A new future awaits us. The time is here, the moment is now.

One of the Founding Fathers of our nation, Thomas Paine, spoke words that apply to all of us gathered here today. They apply directly to all sitting here

in this room. He said, "We have it in our power to begin the world over again."
Thank you. God bless you.

Note: The president spoke at 10:31 a.m. in the General Assembly Hall of the United Nations Headquarters Building. Upon arrival at the United Nations, the president was greeted by Secretary-General Perez de Cuellar. He then met with Paul Lusaka, president of the thirty-ninth session of the General Assembly, who introduced the president to the session.

Following his address, the president returned to the Waldorf-Astoria Hotel, where he met with Prince Norodom Sihanouk and Son Sann of Kampuchea. Before returning to Washington, D.C., the president also met at the hotel with Senator Howard H. Baker, Jr.

NOTE

1. White House correction.

Appendix B

The General Assembly,

Recalling its resolutions 2346 A (XXII) of 19 December 1967, 2153 A (XXI) of 17 November 1966, 2149 (XXI) of 4 November 1966, 2028 (XX) of 19 November 1965 and 1665 (XVI) of 4 December 1961,

Convinced of the urgency and great importance of preventing the spread of nuclear weapons and of intensifying international co-operation in the development of peaceful applications of atomic energy,

Having considered the report of the Conference of the Eighteen-Nation Committee on Disarmament, dated 14 March 1968,[1] and appreciative of the work of the Committee on the elaboration of the draft nonproliferation treaty, which is attached to that report,[2]

Convinced that, pursuant to the provisions of the treaty, all signatories have the right to engage in research, production and use of nuclear energy for peaceful purposes and will be able to acquire source and special fissionable materials, as well as equipment for the processing, use and production of nuclear material for peaceful purposes,

Convinced further that an agreement to prevent the further proliferation of nuclear weapons must be followed as soon as possible by effective measures on the cessation of the nuclear arms race and on nuclear disarmament, and that the nonproliferation treaty will contribute to this aim,

Affirming that in the interest of international peace and security both nuclear-weapon and non-nuclear-weapon States carry the responsibility of acting in accordance with the principles of the Charter of the United Nations that the sovereign equality of all States shall be respected, that the threat or use of force in international relations shall be refrained from and that international disputes shall be settled by peaceful means,

1. *Commends* the Treaty on the Nonproliferation of Nuclear Weapons, the text of which is annexed to the present resolution;

2. *Requests* the Depositary Governments to open the Treaty for signature and ratification at the earliest possible dates;

3. *Expresses the hope* for the widest possible adherence to the Treaty by both nuclear-weapon and non-nuclear-weapon States;

4. *Requests* the Conference of the Eighteen-Nation Committee on Disarmament and the nuclear-weapon States urgently to pursue negotiations on effective measures relating to the cessation of the nuclear arms race at an early date and to nuclear disarmament, and on a treaty on general and complete disarmament under strict and effective international control;

5. *Requests* the Conference of the Eighteen-Nation Committee on Disarmament to report on the progress of its work to the General Assembly at its twenty-third session.

1672nd plenary meeting,
12 June 1968.

ANNEX

Treaty on the Nonproliferation of Nuclear Weapons

The States concluding this Treaty, hereinafter referred to as the "Parties to the Treaty,"

Considering the devastation that would be visited upon all mankind by a nuclear war and the consequent need to make every effort to avert the danger of such a war and to take measures to safeguard the security of peoples,

Believing that the proliferation of nuclear weapons would seriously enhance the danger of nuclear war,

In conformity with resolutions of the United Nations General Assembly calling for the conclusion of an agreement on the prevention of wider dissemination of nuclear weapons,

Undertaking to co-operate in facilitating the application of International Atomic Energy Agency safeguards on peaceful nuclear activities,

Expressing their support for research, development and other efforts to further the application, within the framework of the International Atomic Energy Agency safeguards system, of the principle of safeguarding effectively the flow of source and special fissionable materials by use of instruments and other techniques at certain strategic points,

Affirming the principle that the benefits of peaceful applications of nuclear technology, including any technological by-products which may be derived by nuclear-weapon States from the development of nuclear explosive devices, should be available for peaceful purposes to all Parties to the Treaty, whether nuclear-weapon or non-nuclear-weapon States,

Convinced that, in furtherance of this principle, all Parties to the Treaty are entitled to participate in the fullest possible exchange of scientific information for, and to contribute alone or in co-operation with other States to, the further development of the applications of atomic energy for peaceful purposes,

Declaring their intention to achieve at the earliest possible date the cessation of the nuclear arms race and to undertake effective measures in the direction of nuclear disarmament,

Urging the co-operation of all States in the attainment of this objective,

Recalling the determination expressed by the Parties to the 1963 Treaty banning nuclear weapon tests in the atmosphere, in outer space and under water in its Preamble to seek to achieve the discontinuance of all test explosions of nuclear weapons for all time and to continue negotiations to this end,

Desiring to further the easing of international tension and the strengthening of trust between States in order to facilitate the cessation of the manufacture of nuclear weapons, the liquidation of all their existing stockpiles, and the elimination from national arsenals of nuclear weapons and the means of their delivery pursuant to a treaty on general and complete disarmament under strict and effective international control,

Recalling that, in accordance with the Charter of the United Nations, States must refrain in their international relations from the threat or use of force against the territorial integrity or political independence of any State, or in any other manner inconsistent with the Purposes of the United Nations, and that the establishment and maintenance of international peace and security are to be promoted with the least diversion for armaments of the world's human and economic resources,

Have agreed as follows:

Article I

Each nuclear-weapon State Party to the Treaty undertakes not to transfer to any recipient whatsoever nuclear weapons or other nuclear explosive devices or control over such weapons or explosive devices directly, or indirectly; and not in any way to assist, encourage, or induce any non-nuclear-weapon State to manufacture or otherwise acquire nuclear weapons or other nuclear explosive devices, or control over such weapons or explosive devices.

Article II

Each non-nuclear-weapon State Party to the Treaty undertakes not to receive the transfer from any transferor whatsoever of nuclear weapons or other nuclear explosive devices or of control over such weapons or explosive devices directly, or indirectly; not to manufacture or otherwise acquire nuclear weapons or other nuclear explosive devices; and not to seek or receive any assistance in the manufacture of nuclear weapons or other nuclear explosive devices.

Article III

1. Each non-nuclear-weapon State Party to the Treaty undertakes to accept safeguards, as set forth in an agreement to be negotiated and concluded with

the International Atomic Energy Agency in accordance with the Statute of the International Atomic Energy Agency and the Agency's safeguards system, for the exclusive purpose of verification of the fulfillment of its obligations assumed under this Treaty with a view to preventing diversion of nuclear energy from peaceful uses to nuclear weapons or other nuclear explosive devices. Procedures for the safeguards required by this article shall be followed with respect to source of special fissionable material whether it is being produced, processed or used in any principal nuclear facility or is outside any such facility. The safeguards required by this article shall be applied on all source or special fissionable material in all peaceful nuclear activities within the territory of such State, under its jurisdiction, or carried out under its control anywhere.

2. Each State Party to the Treaty undertakes not to provide: (a) source or special fissionable material, or (b) equipment or material especially designed or prepared for the processing, use or production of special fissionable material, to any non-nuclear-weapon State for peaceful purposes, unless the source or special fissionable material shall be subject to the safeguards required by this article.

3. The safeguards required by this article shall be implemented in a manner designed to comply with article IV of this Treaty, and to avoid hampering the economic or technological development of the Parties or international co-operation in the field of peaceful nuclear activities, including the international exchange of nuclear material and equipment for the processing, use or production of nuclear material for peaceful purposes in accordance with the provisions of this article and the principle of safeguarding set forth in the Preamble of the Treaty.

4. Non-nuclear-weapon States Party to the Treaty shall conclude agreements with the International Atomic Energy Agency to meet the requirements of this article either individually or together with other States in accordance with the Statute of the International Atomic Energy Agency. Negotiation of such agreements shall commence within 180 days from the original entry into force of this Treaty. For States depositing their instruments of ratification or accession after the 180-day period, negotiation of such agreements shall commence not later than the date of such deposit. Such agreements shall enter into force not later than eighteen months after the date of initiation of negotiations.

Article IV

1. Nothing in this Treaty shall be interpreted as affecting the inalienable right of all the Parties to the Treaty to develop research, production and use of nuclear energy for peaceful purposes without discrimination and in conformity with articles I and II of this Treaty.

2. All the Parties to the Treaty undertake to facilitate, and have the right to participate in, the fullest possible exchange of equipment, materials and scientific and technological information for the peaceful uses of nuclear energy. Parties to the Treaty in a position to do so shall also co-operate in contributing alone or together with other States or international organizations to the further development of the applications of nuclear energy for peaceful purposes, especially in the territories of non-nuclear-weapon States Party to the Treaty, with due consideration for the needs of the developing areas of the world.

Article V

Each Party to the Treaty undertakes to take appropriate measures to ensure that, in accordance with this Treaty, under appropriate international observation and through appropriate international procedures, potential benefits from any peaceful applications of nuclear explosions will be made available to non-nuclear-weapon States Party to the Treaty on a non-discriminatory basis and that the charge to such Parties for the explosive devices used will be as low as possible and exclude any charge for research and development. Non-nuclear-weapon States Party to the Treaty shall be able to obtain such benefits, pursuant to a special international agreement or agreements, through an appropriate international body with adequate representation of non-nuclear-weapon States. Negotiations on this subject shall commence as soon as possible after the Treaty enters into force. Non-nuclear-weapon States Party to the Treaty so desiring may also obtain such benefits pursuant to bilateral agreements.

Article VI

Each of the Parties to the Treaty undertakes to pursue negotiations in good faith on effective measures relating to cessation of the nuclear arms race at an early date and to nuclear disarmament, and on a treaty on general and complete disarmament under strict and effective international control.

Article VII

Nothing in this Treaty affects the right of any group of States to conclude regional treaties in order to assure the total absence of nuclear weapons in their respective territories.

Article VIII

1. Any Party to the Treaty may propose amendments to this Treaty. The text of any proposed amendment shall be submitted to the Depositary Governments which shall circulate it to all Parties to the Treaty. Thereupon, if requested to do so by one third or more of the Parties to the Treaty, the Depositary Governments shall convene a conference, to which they shall invite all the Parties to the Treaty, to consider such an amendment.

2. Any amendment to this Treaty must be approved by a majority of the votes of all the Parties to the Treaty, including the votes of all nuclear-weapon States Party to the Treaty and all other Parties which, on the date the amendment is circulated, are members of the Board of Governors of the International Atomic Energy Agency. The amendment shall enter into force for each Party that deposits its instrument of ratification of the amendment upon the deposit of such instruments of ratification by a majority of all the Parties, including the instruments of ratification of all nuclear-weapon States Party to the Treaty and all other Parties which, on the date the amendment is circulated, are members of the Board of Governors of the International Atomic Energy Agency. Thereafter, it shall enter into force for any other Party upon the deposit of its instrument of ratification of the amendment.

3. Five years after the entry into force of this Treaty, a conference of Parties to the Treaty shall be held in Geneva, Switzerland, in order to review the operation of this Treaty with a view to assuring that the purposes of the Preamble and the provisions of the Treaty are being realized. At intervals of five years thereafter, a majority of the Parties to the Treaty may obtain, by submitting a proposal to this effect to the Depositary Governments, the convening of further conferences with the same objective of reviewing the operation of the Treaty.

Article IX

1. This Treaty shall be open to all States for signature. Any State which does not sign the Treaty before its entry into force in accordance with paragraph 3 of this article may accede to it at any time.

2. This Treaty shall be subject to ratification by signatory States. Instruments of ratification and instruments of accession shall be deposited with the Governments of the Union of Soviet Socialist Republics, the United Kingdom of Great Britain and Northern Ireland and the United States of America, which are hereby designated the Depositary Governments.

3. This Treaty shall enter into force after its ratification by the States, the Governments of which are designated Depositaries of the Treaty, and forty other States signatory to this Treaty and the deposit of their instruments of ratification. For the purposes of this Treaty, a nuclear-weapon State is one which has manufactured and exploded a nuclear weapon or other nuclear explosive device prior to 1 January 1967.

4. For States whose instruments of ratification or accession are deposited subsequent to the entry into force of this Treaty, it shall enter into force on the date of the deposit of their instruments of ratification or accession.

5. The Depositary Governments shall promptly inform all signatory and acceding States of the date of each signature, the date of deposit of each instrument of ratification or of accession, the date of the entry into force of this Treaty, and the date of receipt of any requests for convening a conference or other notices.

6. This Treaty shall be registered by the Depositary Governments pursuant to article 102 of the Charter of the United Nations.

Article X

1. Each Party shall in exercising its national sovereignty have the right to withdraw from the Treaty if it decides that extraordinary events, related to the subject-matter of this Treaty, have jeopardized the supreme interests of its country. It shall give notice of such withdrawal to all other Parties to the Treaty and to the United Nations Security Council three months in advance. Such notice shall include a statement of the extraordinary events it regards as having jeopardized its supreme interests.

2. Twenty-five years after the entry into force of the Treaty, a conference shall be convened to decide whether the Treaty shall continue in force indefinitely, or shall be extended for an additional fixed period or periods. This decision shall be taken by a majority of the Parties to the Treaty.

Article XI

This Treaty, the Chinese, English, French, Russian and Spanish texts of which are equally authentic, shall be deposited in the archives of the Depositary Governments. Duly certified copies of this Treaty shall be transmitted by the Depositary Governments to the Governments of the signatory and acceding States.

In witness whereof the undersigned, duly authorized, have signed this Treaty.

Done in . . . this . . . day of . . . .[3]

NOTES

1. United Nations, *Official Records of the General Assembly, Twenty-second Session. Annexes,* agenda item 28, document A/7072-DC/230 (1968).
2. Ibid., annex I.
3. The Treaty was signed in London, Moscow, and Washington on July 1, 1968.

Appendix C

TREATY FOR THE PROHIBITION OF NUCLEAR WEAPONS IN LATIN AMERICA, [Done at Mexico City, February 14, 1967]

Preamble

In the name of their peoples and faithfully interpreting their desires and aspirations, the Governments of the States which have signed the Treaty for the Prohibition of Nuclear Weapons in Latin America,

Desiring to contribute, so far as lies in their power, towards ending the armaments race, especially in the field of nuclear weapons, and towards strengthening a world at peace, based on the sovereign equality of States, mutual respect and good neighbourliness,

Recalling that the United Nations General Assembly, in its resolution 808 (IX), adopted unanimously as one of the three points of a co-ordinated programme of disarmament "the total prohibition of the use and manufacture of nuclear weapons and weapons of mass destruction of every type,"

Recalling that militarily denuclearized zones are not an end in themselves but rather a means for achieving general and complete disarmament at a later stage,

Recalling United Nations General Assembly resolution 1911 (XVIII), which established that the measures that should be agreed upon for the denuclearization

Note: Reproduced from United Nations, *The United Nations and Disarmament—1945–1965* (67.I.8), 1967, pp. 309–322. The treaty was signed on February 14, 1967, by Bolivia, Colombia, Costa Rica, Chile, Ecuador, El Salvador, Guatemala, Haiti, Honduras, Mexico, Panama, Peru, Uruguay, and Venezuela. Nicaragua signed the treaty on February 15, Paraguay signed on April 26, and Brazil signed on May 9, 1967.

of Latin America should be taken "in the light of the principles of the Charter of the United Nations and of regional agreements,"

Recalling United Nations General Assembly resolution 2028 (XX), which established the principle of an acceptable balance of mutual responsibilities and duties for the nuclear and non-nuclear powers, and

Recalling that the Charter of the Organization of American States proclaims that it is an essential purpose of the organization to strengthen the peace and security of the hemisphere,

Convinced:

That the incalculable destructive power of nuclear weapons has made it imperative that the legal prohibition of war should be strictly observed in practice if the survival of civilization and of mankind itself is to be assured,

That nuclear weapons, whose terrible effects are suffered, indiscriminately and inexorably, by military forces and civilian population alike, constitute, through the persistence of the radioactivity they release, an attack on the integrity of the human species and ultimately may even render the whole earth uninhabitable,

That general and complete disarmament under effective international control is a vital matter which all the peoples of the world equally demand,

That the proliferation of nuclear weapons, which seems inevitable unless States, in the exercise of their sovereign rights, impose restrictions on themselves in order to prevent it, would make any agreement on disarmament enormously difficult and would increase the danger of the outbreak of a nuclear conflagration,

That the establishment of militarily denuclearized zones is closely linked with the maintenance of peace and security in the respective regions,

That the military denuclearization of vast geographical zones, adopted by the sovereign decision of the States comprised therein, will exercise a beneficial influence on other regions where similar conditions exist,

That the privileged situation of the signatory States, whose territories are wholly free from nuclear weapons, imposes upon them the inescapable duty of preserving that situation both in their own interests and for the good of mankind,

That the existence of nuclear weapons in any country of Latin America would make it a target for possible nuclear attacks and would inevitably set off, throughout the region, a ruinous race in nuclear weapons which would involve the unjustifiable diversion, for warlike purposes, of the resources required for economic and social development,

That the foregoing reasons, together with the traditional peace-loving outlook of Latin America, give rise to an inescapable necessity that nuclear energy should be used in that region exclusively for peaceful purposes, and that the Latin American countries should use their right to the greatest and most equitable possible access to this new source of energy in order to expedite the economic and social development of their peoples,

Convinced finally:

That the military denuclearization of Latin America—being understood to mean the undertaking entered into internationally in this Treaty to keep their territories forever free from nuclear weapons—will constitute a measure which will spare their peoples from the squandering of their limited resources on nuclear armaments and will protect them against possible nuclear attacks on their territories, and will also constitute a significant contribution towards preventing the proliferation of nuclear weapons and a powerful factor for general and complete disarmament, and

That Latin America, faithful to its tradition of universality, must not only endeavour to banish from its homelands the scourge of a nuclear war, but must also strive to promote the well-being and advancement of its peoples, at the same time co-operating in the fulfillment of the ideals of mankind, that is to say, in the consolidation of a permanent peace based on equal rights, economic fairness and social justice for all, in accordance with the principles and purposes set forth in the Charter of the United Nations and in the Charter of the Organization of American States,

Have agreed as follows:

Obligations

Article 1

1. The contracting Parties hereby undertake to use exclusively for peaceful purposes the nuclear material and facilities which are under their jurisdiction, and to prohibit and prevent in their respective territories:

   (a) The testing, use, manufacture, production or acquisition by any means whatsoever of any nuclear weapons, by the Parties themselves, directly or indirectly, on behalf of anyone else or in any other way; and

   (b) The receipt, storage, installation, deployment and any form of possession of any nuclear weapon, directly or indirectly, by the Parties themselves, by anyone on their behalf or in any other way.

2. The Contracting Parties also undertake to refrain from engaging in, encouraging or authorizing, directly or indirectly, or in any way participating in the testing, use, manufacture, production, possession or control of any nuclear weapon.

Definition of the Contracting Parties

Article 2

For the purposes of this Treaty, the Contracting Parties are those for whom the Treaty is in force.

Definition of territory

Article 3

For the purposes of this Treaty, the term "territory" shall include the territorial sea, air space and any other space over which the State exercises sovereignty in accordance with its own legislation.

Zone of application

Article 4

1. The zone of application of the Treaty is the whole of the territories for which the Treaty is in force.

2. Upon fulfillment of the requirements of article 28, paragraph 1, the zone of application of the Treaty shall also be that which is situated in the western hemisphere within the following limits (except the continental part of the territory of the United States of America and its territorial waters): starting at a point located at 35° north latitude, 75° west longitude; from this point directly southward to a point at 30° north latitude, 75° west longitude; from there, directly

eastward to a point at 30° north latitude, 50° west longitude; from there along a loxodromic line to a point at 5° north latitude, 20° west longitude; from there directly southward to a point at 60° south latitude, 20° west longitude; from there directly westward to a point at 60° south latitude, 115° west longitude; from there directly northward to a point at 0° latitude, 115° west longitude; from there along a loxodromic line to a point at 35° north latitude, 150° west longitude; from there directly eastward to a point at 35° north latitude, 75° west longitude.

Definition of nuclear weapons

Article 5

For the purposes of this Treaty, a nuclear weapon is any device which is capable of releasing nuclear energy in an uncontrolled manner and which has a group of characteristics that are appropriate for use for warlike purposes. An instrument that may be used for the transport or propulsion of the device is not included in this definition if it is separable from the device and not an indivisible part thereof.

Meeting of signatories

Article 6

At the request of any of the signatories, or if the Agency established by article 7 should so decide, a meeting of all the signatories may be convoked to consider in common questions which may affect the very essence of this instrument, including possible amendments to it. In either case, the meeting will be convoked by the General Secretary.

Organization

Article 7

1. In order to ensure compliance with the obligations of this Treaty, the Contracting Parties hereby establish an international organization to be known as the "Agency for the Prohibition of Nuclear Weapons in Latin America," hereinafter referred to as "the Agency." Only the Contracting Parties shall be affected by its decisions.

2. The Agency shall be responsible for the holding of periodic or extraordinary consultations among member States on matters relating to the purposes, measures and procedures set forth in this Treaty and to supervision of compliance with the obligations arising there from.

3. The Contracting Parties agree to extend to the Agency full and prompt cooperation in accordance with the provisions of this Treaty, of any agreements they may conclude with the Agency and of any agreements the Agency may conclude with any other international organization or body.

4. The headquarters of the Agency shall be in Mexico City.

Organs

Article 8

1. There are hereby established as principal organs of the Agency a General Conference, a Council and a Secretariat.

2. Such subsidiary organs as are considered necessary by the General Conference may be established within the purview of this Treaty.

The General Conference

Article 9

1. The General Conference, the supreme organ of the Agency, shall be composed of all the Contracting Parties; it shall hold regular sessions every two years, and may also hold special sessions whenever this Treaty so provides, or, in the opinion of the Council, the circumstances so require.

2. The General Conference:

   (a) May consider and decide on matters or questions covered by the Treaty, within the limits thereof, including those referring to powers and functions of any organ provided for in this Treaty.

   (b) Shall establish procedures for the control system to ensure observance of this Treaty in accordance with its provisions.

   (c) Shall elect the members of the Council and the General Secretary.

   (d) May remove the General Secretary from office if the proper functioning of the Agency so requires.

   (e) Shall receive and consider the biennial and special reports submitted by the Council and the General Secretary.

   (f) Shall initiate and consider studies designed to facilitate the optimum fulfillment of the aims of this Treaty, without prejudice to the power of the General Secretary independently to carry out similar studies for submission to and consideration by the Conference.

   (g) Shall be the organ competent to authorize the conclusion of agreements with Governments and other international organizations and bodies.

3. The General Conference shall adopt the Agency's budget and fix the scale of financial contributions to be paid by member States, taking into account the systems and criteria used for the same purpose by the United Nations.

4. The General Conference shall elect its officers for each session and may establish such subsidiary organs as it deems necessary for the performance of its functions.

5. Each member of the Agency shall have one vote. The decisions of the General Conference shall be taken by a two-thirds majority of the members present and voting in the case of matters relating to the control system and measures referred to in article 20, the admission of new members, the election or removal of the General Secretary, adoption of the budget and matters related thereto. Decisions on other matters, as well as procedural questions, and also determination of which questions must be decided by a two-thirds majority, shall be taken by a simple majority of the members present and voting.

6. The General Conference shall adopt its own rules of procedure.

The Council

Article 10

1. The Council shall be composed of five members of the Agency elected by the General Conference from among the Contracting Parties, due account being taken of equitable geographical distribution.

2. The members of the Council shall be elected for a term of four years. However, in the first election three will be elected for two years. Outgoing members may not be re-elected for the following period unless the limited number of States for which the Treaty is in force so requires.

3. Each member of the Council shall have one representative.

4. The Council shall be so organized as to be able to function continuously.

5. In addition to the functions conferred upon it by this Treaty and to those which may be assigned to it by the General Conference, the Council shall, through the General Secretary, ensure the proper operation of the control system in accordance with the provisions of this Treaty and with the decisions adopted by the General Conference.

6. The Council shall submit an annual report on its work to the General Conference as well as such special reports as it deems necessary or which the General Conference requests of it.

7. The Council shall elect its officers for each session.

8. The decisions of the Council shall be taken by a simple majority of its members present and voting.

9. The Council shall adopt its own rules of procedure.

The Secretariat

Article 11

1. The Secretariat shall consist of a General Secretary, who shall be the chief administrative officer of the Agency, and of such staff as the Agency may require. The term of office of the General Secretary shall be four years and he may be re-elected for a single additional term. The General Secretary may not be a national of the country in which the Agency has its headquarters. In case the office of General Secretary becomes vacant, a new election shall be held to fill the office for the remainder of the term.

2. The staff of the Secretariat shall be appointed by the General Secretary, in accordance with rules laid down by the General Conference.

3. In addition to the functions conferred upon him by this Treaty and to those which may be assigned to him by the General Conference, the General Secretary shall ensure, as provided by article 10, paragraph 5, the proper operation of the control system established by this Treaty, in accordance with the provisions of the Treaty and the decisions taken by the General Conference.

4. The General Secretary shall act in that capacity in all meetings of the General Conference and of the Council and shall make an annual report to both bodies on the work of the Agency and any special reports requested by the General Conference or the Council or which the General Secretary may deem desirable.

5. The General Secretary shall establish the procedures for distributing to all Contracting Parties information received by the Agency from governmental sources, and such information from non-governmental sources as may be of interest to the Agency.

6. In the performance of their duties, the General Secretary and the staff shall not seek or receive instructions from any Government or from any other authority external to the Agency and shall refrain from any action which might reflect on their position as international officials responsible only to the Agency; subject to their responsibility to the Agency, they shall not disclose any industrial secrets or other confidential information coming to their knowledge by reason of their official duties in the Agency.

7. Each of the Contracting Parties undertakes to respect the exclusively international character of the responsibilities of the General Secretary and the staff and not to seek to influence them in the discharge of their responsibilities.

Control system

Article 12

1. For the purpose of verifying compliance with the obligations entered into by the Contracting Parties in accordance with article 1, a control system shall be established which shall be put into effect in accordance with the provisions of articles 13–18 of this Treaty.

2. The control system shall be used in particular for the purpose of verifying:

(a) That devices, services and facilities intended for peaceful uses of nuclear energy are not used in the testing or manufacture of nuclear weapons;

(b) That none of the activities prohibited in article 1 of this Treaty are carried out in the territory of the Contracting Parties with nuclear materials or weapons introduced from abroad, and

(c) That explosions for peaceful purposes are compatible with article 18 of this Treaty.

IAEA safeguards

Article 13

Each Contracting Party shall negotiate multilateral or bilateral agreements with the International Atomic Energy Agency for the application of its safeguards to its nuclear activities. Each Contracting Party shall initiate negotiations within a period of 180 days after the date of the deposit of its instrument of ratification of this Treaty. These agreements shall enter into force, for each Party, not later than eighteen months after the date of the initiation of such negotiations except in case of unforeseen circumstances or *force majeure.*

Reports of the parties

Article 14

1. The Contracting Parties shall submit to the Agency and to the International Atomic Energy Agency, for their information, semi-annual reports stating that no activity prohibited under this Treaty has occurred in their respective territories.

2. The Contracting Parties shall simultaneously transmit to the Agency a copy of any report they may submit to the International Atomic Energy Agency which relates to matters that are the subject of this Treaty and to the application of safeguards.

3. The Contracting Parties shall also transmit to the Organization of American States, for its information, any reports that may be of interest to it, in accordance with the obligations established by the Inter-American System.

Special reports requested by the General Secretary

Article 15

1. With the authorization of the Council, the General Secretary may request any of the Contracting Parties to provide the Agency with complementary or supplementary information regarding any event or circumstance connected with compliance with this Treaty, explaining his reasons. The Contracting Parties undertake to co-operate promptly and fully with the General Secretary.

2. The General Secretary shall inform the Council and the Contracting Parties forthwith of such requests and of the respective replies.

Special inspections

Article 16

1. The International Atomic Energy Agency and the Council established by this Treaty have the power of carrying out special inspections in the following cases:

(a) In the case of the International Atomic Energy Agency, in accordance with the agreements referred to in article 13 of the Treaty;

(b) In the case of the Council:

(i) When so requested, the reasons for the request being stated, by any Party which suspects that some activity prohibited by this Treaty has been carried out or is about to be carried out, either in the territory of any other Party or in any other place on such latter Party's behalf, the Council shall immediately arrange for such an inspection in accordance with article 10, paragraph 5.

(ii) When requested by any Party which has been suspected of or charged with having violated the Treaty, the Council shall immediately arrange for the special inspection requested, in accordance with article 10, paragraph 5.

The above requests will be made to the Council through the General Secretary.

2. The costs and expenses of any special inspection carried out under paragraph 1, sub-paragraph (b), sections (i) and (ii) of this article shall be borne by the requesting Party or Parties, except where the Council concludes on the basis of the report on the special inspection that, in view of the circumstances existing in the case, such costs and expenses should be borne by the Agency.

3. The General Conference shall formulate the procedures for the organization and execution of the special inspections carried out in accordance with paragraph 1, sub-paragraph (b), sections (i) and (ii) of this article.

4. The Contracting Parties undertake to grant the inspectors carrying out such special inspections full and free access to all places and all information which may be necessary for the performance of their duties and which are directly and intimately connected with the suspicion of violation of this Treaty. If so requested by the Contracting Party in whose territory the inspection is carried out, the inspectors designated by the General Conference shall be accompanied by representatives of the authorities of that Contracting Party, provided that this does not in any way delay or hinder the work of the inspectors.

5. The Council shall immediately transmit to all the Parties, through the General Secretary, a copy of any report resulting from special inspections.

6. Similarly, the Council shall send through the General Secretary to the Secretary-General of the United Nations for transmission to the United Nations Security Council and General Assembly, and to the Council of the Organization of American States for its information, a copy of any report resulting from any special inspection carried out in accordance with paragraph 1, sub-paragraph (b), sections (i) and (ii) of this article.

7. The Council may decide, or any Contracting Party may request, the convening of a special session of the General Conference for the purpose of considering the reports resulting from any special inspection. In such a case, the General Secretary shall take immediate steps to convene the special session requested.

8. The General Conference, convened in special session under this article, may make recommendations to the Contracting Parties and submit reports to the Secretary-General of the United Nations to be transmitted to the Security Council and the General Assembly.

Use of nuclear energy for peaceful purposes
Article 17
Nothing in the provisions of this Treaty shall prejudice the rights of the Contracting Parties, in conformity with this Treaty, to use nuclear energy for peaceful purposes, in particular for their economic development and social progress.

Explosions for peaceful purposes
Article 18
1. The Contracting Parties may carry out explosions of nuclear devices for peaceful purposes – including explosions which involve devices similar to those used in nuclear weapons – or collaborate with third parties for the same purpose, provided that they do so in accordance with the provisions of this article and the other articles of the Treaty, particularly articles 1 and 5.

2. Contracting Parties intending to carry out, or co-operate in the carrying out of such an explosion shall notify the Agency and the International Atomic Energy Agency, as far in advance as the circumstances require, of the date of the explosion and shall at the same time provide the following information:
   (a) The nature of the nuclear device and the source from which it was obtained;
   (b) The place and purpose of the planned explosion;
   (c) The procedures which will be followed in order to comply with paragraph 3 of this article;
   (d) The expected force of the device;
   (e) The fullest possible information on any possible radioactive fall-out that
   (e) may result from the explosion or explosions, and the measures which will be taken to avoid danger to the population, flora and fauna, and territories of any other Party or Parties.

3. The General Secretary and the technical personnel designated by the Council and the International Atomic Energy Agency may observe all the preparations, including the explosion of the device, and shall have unrestricted access to any area in the vicinity of the site of the explosion in order to ascertain whether the device and the procedures followed during the explosion are in conformity with the information supplied under paragraph 2 of the present article and the other provisions of this Treaty.

4. The Contracting Parties may accept the collaboration of third parties for the purpose set forth in paragraph 1 of the present article, in accordance with paragraphs 2 and 3 thereof.

Relations with other international organizations
Article 19
1. The Agency may conclude such agreements with the International Atomic Energy Agency as are authorized by the General Conference and as it considers likely to facilitate the efficient operation of the control system established by this Treaty.

2. The Agency may also enter into relations with any international organization or body, especially any which may be established in the future to supervise disarmament or measures for the control of armaments in any part of the world.

3. The Contracting Parties may, if they see fit, request the advice of the Inter-American Nuclear Energy Commission on all technical matters connected with the application of the Treaty with which the Commission is competent to deal under its Statute.

Measures in the event of violation of the Treaty
Article 20

1. The General Conference shall take note of all cases in which, in its opinion, any Contracting Party is not complying fully with its obligations under this Treaty and shall draw the matter to the attention of the Party concerned, making such recommendations as it deems appropriate.

2. If, in its opinion, such non-compliance constitutes a violation of this Treaty which might endanger peace and security, the General Conference shall report thereon simultaneously to the Security Council and the General Assembly through the Secretary-General of the United Nations and to the Council of the Organization of American States. The General Conference shall likewise report to the International Atomic Energy Agency for such purposes as are relevant in accordance with its Statute.

United Nations and Organization of American States
Article 21

None of the provisions of this Treaty shall be construed as impairing the rights and obligations of the Parties under the Charter of the United Nations or, in the case of States members of the Organization of American States, under existing regional treaties.

Privileges and immunities
Article 22

1. The Agency shall enjoy in the territory of each of the Contracting Parties such legal capacity and such privileges and immunities as may be necessary for the exercise of its functions and the fulfillment of its purposes.

2. Representatives of the Contracting Parties accredited to the Agency and officials of the Agency shall similarly enjoy such privileges and immunities as are necessary for the performance of their functions.

3. The Agency may conclude agreements with the Contracting Parties with a view to determining the details of the application of paragraphs 1 and 2 of this article.

Notification of other agreements
Article 23

Once this Treaty has entered into force, the Secretariat shall be notified immediately of any international agreement concluded by any of the Contracting Parties on matters with which this Treaty is concerned; the Secretariat shall register it and notify the other Contracting Parties.

Settlement of disputes
Article 24

Unless the Parties concerned agree on another mode of peaceful settlement, any question or dispute concerning the interpretation or application of this Treaty which is not settled shall be referred to the International Court of Justice with the prior consent of the parties to the controversy.

Signature
Article 25

1. This Treaty shall be open indefinitely for signature by:

(a) All the Latin American Republics;

(b) All other sovereign States situated in their entirety south of latitude 35° north in the western hemisphere; and, except as provided in paragraph 2 of this article, all such States which become sovereign, when they have been admitted by the General Conference.

2. The General Conference shall not take any decision regarding the admission of a political entity part or all of whose territory is the subject, prior to the date when this Treaty is opened for signature, of a dispute or claim between an extra-continental country and one or more Latin American States, so long as the dispute has not been settled by peaceful means.

Ratification and deposit

Article 26

1. This Treaty shall be subject to ratification by signatory States in accordance with their respective constitutional procedures.

2. This Treaty and the instruments of ratification shall be deposited with the Government of the United States of Mexico, which is hereby designated the Depositary Government.

3. The Depositary Government shall send certified copies of this Treaty to the Governments of signatory States and shall notify them of the deposit of each instrument of ratification.

Reservations

Article 27

This Treaty shall not be subject to reservations.

Entry into force

Article 28

1. Subject to the provisions of paragraph 2 and 3 of this article, this Treaty shall enter into force among the States that have ratified it as soon as the following requirements have been met:

(a) Deposit of the instruments of ratification of this Treaty with the Depositary Government by the Governments of the States mentioned in article 25 which are in existence on the date when this Treaty is opened for signature and which are not affected by the provisions of article 25, paragraph 2;

(b) Signature and ratification of Additional Protocol I annexed to this Treaty by all extra-continental and continental States having *de jure* or *de facto* international responsibility of territories situated in the zone of application of the Treaty;

(c) Signature and ratification of the Additional Protocol II annexed to this Treaty by all powers possessing nuclear weapons;

(d) Conclusion of bilateral agreements on the application of the Safeguards System of the International Atomic Energy Agency in accordance with article 13 of this Treaty.

2. All signatory States shall have the imprescriptible right to waive, wholly or in part, the requirements laid down in the preceding paragraph. They may do so by means of a declaration which shall be annexed to their respective instruments of ratification and which may be formulated at the time of deposit of the instrument or subsequently. For those States which exercise this right, this Treaty shall enter into force upon deposit of the declaration, or as soon as those requirements have been met which have not been expressly waived.

3. As soon as this Treaty has entered into force in accordance with the provisions of paragraph 2 for eleven States, the Depositary Government shall convene a preliminary meeting of those States in order that the Agency may be set up and commence its work.

4. After the entry into force of the Treaty for all the countries of the zone, the rise of a new power possessing nuclear weapons shall have the effect of suspending the execution of this Treaty for those countries which have ratified it without waiving the requirements of paragraph 1, sub-paragraph (c) of this article, and which request such suspension; the Treaty shall remain suspended until the new power, on its own initiative or upon request by the General Conference, ratifies the annexed Additional Protocol II.

Amendments

Article 29

1. Any Contracting Party may propose amendments to this Treaty and shall submit their proposals to the Council through the General Secretary, who shall transmit them to all the other Contracting Parties and, in addition, to signatories in accordance with article 6. The Council, through the General Secretary, shall, immediately following the meeting of signatories, convene a special session of the General Conference to examine the proposals made, for the adoption of which a two-thirds majority of the Contracting Parties present and voting shall be required.

2. Amendments adopted shall enter into force as soon as the requirements set forth in article 28 of this Treaty have been complied with.

Duration and denunciation

Article 30

1. This Treaty shall be of permanent nature and shall remain in force indefinitely, but any Party may denounce it by notifying the General Secretary of the Agency if, in the opinion of the denouncing State, there have arisen or may arise circumstances connected with the content of the Treaty or of the annexed Additional Protocols I and II which affect its supreme interests and the peace and security of one or more Contracting Parties.

2. The denunciation shall take effect three months after the delivery to the General Secretary of the Agency of the notification by the Government of the signatory State concerned. The General Secretary shall immediately communicate such notification to the other Contracting Parties and to the Secretary-General of the United Nations for the information of the Security Council and the General Assembly of the United Nations. He shall also communicate it to the Secretary General of the Organization of American States.

Authentic texts and registration

Article 31

This Treaty, of which the Spanish, Chinese, English, French, Portuguese and Russian texts are equally authentic, shall be registered by the Depositary Government in accordance with Article 102 of the United Nations Charter. The Depositary Government shall notify the Secretary-General of the United Nations of the signatures, ratifications and amendments relating to this Treaty and shall communicate them to the Secretary General of the Organization of American States for his information.

Transitional Article

Denunciation of the declaration referred to in article 28, paragraph 2, shall be subject to the same procedures as the denunciation of the Treaty, except that it shall take effect on the date of delivery of the respective notification.

In witness whereof the undersigned Plenipotentiaries, having deposited their full powers, found in good and due form, sign this Treaty on behalf of their respective Governments.

Done at Mexico City, Distrito Federal, on the fourteenth day of February, one thousand nine hundred and sixty-seven.

Additional Protocol I

The undersigned Plenipotentiaries, furnished with full powers by their respective Governments,

Convinced that the Treaty for the Prohibition of Nuclear Weapons in Latin America, negotiated and signed in accordance with the recommendations of the General Assembly of the United Nations in resolution 1911 (XVIII) of 27 November 1963, represents an important step towards ensuring the nonproliferation of nuclear weapons,

Aware that the nonproliferation of nuclear weapons is not an end in itself but rather a means of achieving general and complete disarmament at a later stage,

Desiring to contribute, so far as lies in their power, towards ending the armaments race, especially in the field of nuclear weapons, and towards strengthening a world at peace, based on mutual respect and sovereign equality of States,

Have agreed as follows:

Article 1. To undertake to apply the status of denuclearization in respect of warlike purposes as defined in articles 1, 3, 5 and 13 of the Treaty for the Prohibition of Nuclear Weapons in Latin America in territories for which, *de jure* or *de facto,* they are internationally responsible and which lie within the limits of the geographical zone established in that Treaty.

Article 2. The duration of this Protocol shall be the same as that of the Treaty for the Prohibition of Nuclear Weapons in Latin America of which this Protocol is an annex, and the provisions regarding ratification and denunciation contained in the Treaty shall be applicable to it.

Article 3. This Protocol shall enter into force, for the States which have ratified it, on the date of the deposit of their respective instruments of ratification.

In witness whereof the undersigned Plenipotentiaries, having deposited their full powers, found in good and due form, sign this Treaty on behalf of their respective Governments.

Additional Protocol II

The undersigned Plenipotentiaries, furnished with full powers by their respective Governments,

Convinced that the Treaty for the Prohibition of Nuclear Weapons in Latin America, negotiated and signed in accordance with the recommendations of the General Assembly of the United Nations in resolution 1911 (XVIII) of 27 November 1963, is an important step towards ensuring the nonproliferation of nuclear weapons,

Aware that the nonproliferation of nuclear weapons is not an end in itself but rather a means for achieving general and complete disarmament at a later stage,

Desiring to contribute, so far as lies in their power, towards ending the armaments race, especially in the field of nuclear weapons, and towards promoting and strengthening a world at peace based on mutual respect and sovereign equality of States,

Have agreed as follows:

Article 1. The status of denuclearization of Latin America in respect of warlike purposes, as defined, delimited and set forth in the Treaty for the Prohibition of Nuclear Weapons in Latin America of which this instrument is an annex, shall be fully respected by the Parties to this Protocol in all its express aims and provisions.

Article 2. The Governments represented by the undersigned Plenipotentiaries undertake, therefore, not to contribute in any way to the performance of acts involving a violation of the obligations of article 1 of the Treaty in the territories to which the Treaty applies in accordance with article 4 thereof.

Article 3. The Governments represented by the undersigned Plenipotentiaries also undertake not to use or threaten to use nuclear weapons against the Contracting Parties of the Treaty for the Prohibition of Nuclear Weapons in Latin America.

Article 4. The duration of this Protocol shall be the same as that of the Treaty for the Prohibition of Nuclear Weapons in Latin America of which this Protocol is an annex, and the definitions of territory and nuclear weapons set forth in articles 3 and 5 of the Treaty shall be applicable to the Protocol, as well as the provisions regarding ratification, reservations, denunciation, authentic texts and registration contained in articles 26, 27, 30 and 31 of the Treaty.

Article 5. This Protocol shall enter into force, for the States which have ratified it, on the date of the deposit of their respective instruments of ratification.

In witness whereof the undersigned Plenipotentiaries, having deposited their full powers, found in good and due form, sign this Treaty on behalf of their respective Governments.

About the Author

Dr. William H. Lewis is director of security policy studies and professor of political science at the George Washington University, Washington, D.C. He served previously with the U.S. Department of State and is the author of several studies on political-military issues.